D1609666

Contents

Dedication

To my family who are always there for me and allow me the space and time to create.

And to my tribe of fellow crafters who make working in this field a never-ending journey of creativity, inspiration and imagination.

With thanks to New Holland Publishers for the fabulous opportunity to share my papercraft projects with you all.

Introduction

Welcome to my first ever papercraft book. I am so excited to be able to share with you all many of my favorite projects, and a few I have developed just for this book. I hope you will be tempted to make them yourself and find the same joy in creating that I do.

I have been a papercraft fan for over 20 years, and have found that there are just about limitless things you can do with ordinary paper, cardstock and recycled items. This book shows that you can make gorgeous 3-D projects to celebrate the seasons through the year and beyond. Many of the projects I make each year with a little variation or twist to suit the recipient or theme. Nothing says you care more than a handmade item, and even more when you can add a personal touch. So feel free to alter and adapt the templates and ideas to suit you, if you do not have the exact tools, dies or materials, substitute what you do have. Sometimes by just changing the color or adding a few flowers, you can change the look and feel of a project dramatically. I have included lots of handy hints to help you add variety to the projects, and make them unique to you.

There are comprehensive material lists and great instructions for you to follow, along with all the templates you will need. What I like to do is print out the templates, adhere them to cardstock, and cut out to make an easy traceable template. The templates for each of the projects can be found at the end of the book. As with all projects, it can be a great idea to make them in plain cardstock first, to work out any of the bugs, before cutting into your very best patterned paper. I hope like me, you find your favorite projects, which you will make over and over again for friends and family in the years to come and that I inspire you to think outside the box and come up with your own 3-D papercraft ideas.

Sue Smyth

FACEBOOK https://www.facebook.com/susanne.smyth.3
BLOG http://suesmyth06.blogspot.com

A Piece of Cake

Make someone's day with this stunning piece of cake, or even make a whole cake for a party centerpiece.

MATERIALS

2 sheets of 30 x 30 cm (12 x 12 in) white cardstock

Doily border punch

Any embossing folder

White pearl paint

2 packs 3 mm self-adhesive pearl strips

3mm self-adhesive pearls

White eyelash fiber

1 red and white straw

Gesso

Dimensional magic

White glitter

Spray adhesive

White muslin

2 paper daisies

Vintage rose glimmer mist

Silver micro beads

Scalloped circle dies

Double sided tape

3-D foam tape

Hot glue gun

Hand die-cutting machine

Yellow alcohol pen

Scrap of acetate

Spray water bottle

STEPS

- Trace around template to create box bottom and lid, score on fold lines and use double sided tape to assemble. You may need a drop of hot glue at the corners for strength.
- Punch doily border from remaining white cardstock, adhere around the bottom edge of the lid of box.
- Cut 2 strips 1 x 30 cm (0.4 x 12 in) of white cardstock, apply dimensional magic over the strips, smooth with fingertip and sprinkle with white glitter. When dry attach over doily border with double sided tape, trimming off excess. Attach medium pearl strip over join.
- Attach smaller pearl strip to the top of the glitter strip.
- Use the top of the lid as a template to cut another triangle shape a little smaller than the top.
- Emboss with extra loren folder, dry brush pearl paint over raised areas, when dry attach to top of lid with 3-D foam tape. Wrap white fiber around the edge of raised panel.
- Die-cut a scalloped circle from white cardstock, cover with dimensional magic, smooth out with fingertip and sprinkle with white glitter. Affix to top of lid with 3-D foam tape.
- Spray large paper rose with adhesive and dip into a pot of white glitter.
- Spray vintage rose spray onto acetate to form a puddle. Spray paper daisies with water and dip into puddle of Vintage rose, so the ink wicks up the petals. Allow to dry. Apply dimensional magic to the centers and sprinkle over silver micro beads.
- Attach flowers to the glittered scalloped circle, tuck in small shards of muslin around the edges.
- Paint straw with gesso, allow to dry, cover straw with dimensional magic and dip into white glitter. Trim to fit into the cluster of flowers.
- Trim out a small wick shape, color with yellow alcohol pen and adhere into the straw candle with hot glue.

•Handy Hint•

You can make these boxes in any color and with different toppers to make a very personalized gift.

Make enough boxes to make a complete cake, arrange on a crystal cake stand for a stunning center piece.

Use grungier darker colors for a more masculine cake.

An Apple a Day

What could be nicer than an apple 3-D mini album for your favorite teacher? Add photos of all the kids for a memorable keepsake.

MATERIALS

2 30 x 30 cm (12 x 12 in) red cardstock
1 10 x 10 cm (4 x 4 in) green & white cardstock
An old book
Scalloped and nested circle dies
Couture Creations strawberry leaf die
Gold paint
Metallic green paint
Small piece of plastic vine or stick
Black eyelash fiber

Alphabet chipboard
Assorted buttons and resin flowers
3mm pearl self-adhesive strips
White glitter
Dimensional magic
Blue, red and yellow stamp pads
Black fine tip pen
Sanding block

STEPS

- Die-cut a large circle from the red cardstock 18 times. Trim the bottom 1 cm off. Fold all circles in half.
- Adhere each folded circle to the next one, layering them up to form a book. Pay attention to line up the spine, you can always trim the edges, but not the spine.
- Rub gold paint over the edges and spine and allow to dry.
- Die-cut photos and old book pages with a small circle die, sand edges and adhere to all of the pages as desired.
- Die-cut a large circle from a book page, trim to shape of apple and adhere to covers, draw in a seed and stitched detail with a fine black pen.
- Die-cut a small scalloped circle from white cardstock. Die-cut a photo with a matching nested die and adhere with 3-D foam tape. Snip pearl strip into 2 pearl lengths and adhere around the photo.
- Tuck and arrange a variety of buttons, gemstones and resin flowers underneath.
- Paint the A, B, C with gesso, ink with yellow, blue and red stamp pads or ink, cover with dimensional magic, smooth out with your fingertip, and sprinkle with a little white glitter.
- Adhere a small piece of plastic vine to the spine of the apple.
- Die-cut 2 leaves, dry brush with green metallic paint, and adhere to either side of the stalk. Wrap with a few black fibers.

•Handy Hint•

You can make a red or green apple, try making a pear shape too for fun.

Leave the album empty so the teacher can fill it with photos of the children in the class.

You can also put all of your child's teachers' photos in the album if you want to make one for yourself.

Make this in orange and it becomes an awesome Halloween pumpkin.

Bird Cage Hanging Decoration

Sweetly scented with cinnamon this gorgeous decoration could hang in your car, wardrobe or even on the Christmas tree.

MATERIALS

1 30 x 30 cm (12 x 12 in) sheet of white cardstock

1 30 x 30 cm (12 x 12 in sheet of lightweight chipboard

1 10 x 10 cm (4 x 4 in) green cardstock

White glitter

Blue glitter

Dimensional magic

2 spotted feathers

Silver micro beads

Night sky and mango dew drops stamp pad

1 medium white paper rose

2 small white paper roses

1 large pink paper rose

Twig punch

3mm self-adhesive pearl strip

Black rhinestones

Muslin

1 large self-adhesive pearls

White organza ribbon

Pearl string

1 cinnamon stick

Gold tassel trim

Heat gun

Hot glue gun

Hand die-cutting machine

Double sided tape

3-D foam tape

Tim Holtz Alterations caged bird die

STEPS

- Die-cut 4 bird cages from white cardstock and two from light weight chipboard. Adhere cardstock cages to either side of the chipboard ones. Apply dimensional magic to the cage, smooth out with your fingertip and sprinkle with white glitter. Allow to dry.
- Trim a small strip of chipboard 6.5 x 5 cm (2.5 x 2 in), score a 1 cm (0.4 in) tab on each side of the 5 cm (2 in) edge to form a base. Adhere base with hot glue to each of the cages.
- Adhere gold tassel trim to the outside base of the cage.
- Punch out 4 leaves from green cardstock, adhere 2 to front of cage and 2 to the back. Layer over large rose and 2 small roses to the front and a single medium rose to the back. Tuck two spotted feathers beside roses on the front.
- Snip up pearl strip into pieces and adhere to front and back of cage with glue, punch a hole in the top of both cages, and adhere a large pearl to both sides.
- Die-cut 2 birds from white cardstock and one from chipboard, adhere white cardstock birds to either side of chipboard. Apply a coat of dimensional magic and smooth out with your fingertip, sprinkle with silver micro beads and allow to dry.
- Coat bird with gesso and dry with heat gun, color bird with night sky and mango inks. Add a small black rhinestone as an eye.
- Die-cut wings, from white cardstock, apply dimensional magic and smooth out with your fingertip, sprinkle with blue glitter, and when dry, attach to the body of the bird.
- Adhere bird and a cinnamon stick to base of cage, add teased muslin around the base to hide the glue.
- Thread pearl string through holes and tie up, add a generous white organza ribbon bow to finish.

•Handy Hint•

Adhere the wings of the bird at the tip only so you can bend them out for dimension like a real bird.

If you don't have a cinnamon stick just add a small stick from the garden.

Do this in Christmas colors for a beautiful tree decoration.

Add a small tag with a birthday greeting to make a sweet gift for a friend.

Use old cereal boxes to cut out the cage and save money.

Birdhouse Sweet Box

Celebrate spring with a quaint birdhouse sweet box, wonderful for any age or gender.

MATERIALS

1 30 x 30 cm (12 x 12 in) in cream cardstock

1 30 x 30 cm (12 x 12 in) in brown cardstock

1 15 x 15 cm (6 x 6 in) white & green cardstock

1 9 x 9 cm (3.5 x 3.5 in) chipboard

2 small pink paper roses

1 small blue paper rose

1 very small pink paper rose

White organza ribbon

2 packs 3mm self-adhesive pearl strips

Twig punch

Fence and doily border punch

Scalloped and nested circle dies

Scalloped squares die

Assorted foliage clear stamps

Olive glimmer dust

Turquoise glimmer mist

Gesso

Gingerbread dew drops stamp pad

Jet black and sepia archival ink stamp pad

Gold spray glitter

Green/brown eyelash fiber

1 medium craft bird

1 small twig

Hot glue gun

Hand die-cutting machine

Double sided tape

3-D foam tape

STEPS

- Trace around template to make bird house base, trim out. Randomly stamp foliage and script stamps around the sides in sepia and black ink, and spritz with glimmer mists. Allow to dry.
- Layer a small circle die over one of the peaked sides of the box and die-cut to create a window. Fold up and assemble box, punch out doily border from white cardstock and adhere to base of bird house, layer over a strip of pearls.
- Cut two 9 x 9 cm (3.5 x 3.5 in) squares of cream cardstock and chipboard. Adhere cream cardstock to either side of chipboard, stamp randomly with script stamp and sepia ink. Ink around the edges.
- Punch out fence border from white cardstock, fold and fit around the chipboard base. Adhere in place with hot glue to all 4 corners. Layer over a strip of pearls.
- Adhere birdhouse to center of base with hot glue, add extra glue to the inside for a strong bond.
- Die-cut a medium scalloped circle from white cardstock, then die-cut a nested circle from the center to create a scalloped frame. Cover with dimensional magic, smooth out with your fingertip and dip into a pot of white glitter, allow to dry and adhere over house window with 3-D foam tape. Wrap eyelash fibers around the edge.
- Adhere a small stick, bird and paper rose to the window as pictured.
- Punch out 4 leaves from green cardstock, adhere 2 to the flowers and bird cluster.
- Cut an 8.5 x 16 cm (3.3 x 6.3 in) panel from cream cardstock and fold in half, hot glue one side to the roof tabs. Leave the other open so you can fill the box with items.
- Die-cut brown cardstock with scalloped square die, no need to do all of the die, just cut brown strips 4 cm wide by 13 cm long (1.5 x 5.1 in) and die-cut the scalloped edge (as this is the only part we use). Die-cut 5 strips.
- Score along each of the scallops over a mouse pad, trim to neaten and adhere starting from the bottom of the roof panel with double sided tape. Finish one side and start at the bottom of the remaining side.
- Use your fingers to furl up the scallops for great dimension. Dry brush with gesso and spray with gold glitter spray.
- Adhere a generous bow, small pink paper rose and the remaining 2 green leaves to the top of the roof.
- Tuck some muslin into the window to hide the center or fill with sweets in a cello bag.

•Handy Hint•

Cover the window with acetate or vellum if you want to fill with small sweets that are loose.

You can make this house hanging by just adding a string through the roof and flower. Add a tassel to finish off below.

This can convert to a spooky house easily by using darker Halloween colors and a bat in the window instead.

Birdie Cylinder Gift Box

A pretty gift box is always a great start to gift giving, this cylinder box can be decorated with any pretty flower and butterfly and filled with sweets or small gifts.

MATERIALS

1 30 x 30 cm (12 x 12 in) white cardstock

1 10 x 10 cm (4 x 4 in) green cardstock

Graphic 45 Secret Garden collection sun-kissed patterned paper

3mm self-adhesive pearl strips

Largeself-adhesive pearl

Small craft bird

White organza ribbon

2 medium white paper roses

1 small pink paper rose

White glitter

Spray adhesive

Wood fiber

Twig punch

Border punch

Nested circle dies

Pearl brad

Small feather die

Lavender stamp pad

small white tassel

1 toilet roll insert

Hot glue gun

Hand die-cutting machine

Double sided tape

Bamboo skewer

STEPS

- Trim patterned paper to fit around toilet roll, adhere in place with double sided tape.
- Punch doily border from white cardstock and attach to both ends, affix pearl strips over top.
- Cut a 2.5 cm (1 in) strip of white cardstock and wrap around middle, layer over organza ribbon, and trim to fit.
- Bunch together a little wood fiber and adhere to top of cylinder, affix bird over top.
- Ink white roses with lavender ink, spray with adhesive and dip into a pot of white glitter.
- Coil up wire stems over a bamboo skewer, adhere along with small pink rose to side of nest.
- Punch 2 green leaves, tuck either side of roses.
- Tie an organza bow, affix to opposite side of nest.
- Die-cut 2 feathers from white cardstock, ink edges with lavender and tuck under bow.
- Die-cut 2 circles that best fit the ends of the cylinder, die-cut 2 smaller circles from patterned paper and adhere over top.
- Trim circles to fit ends of cylinder if needed, affix one end with hot glue. Insert brad to other end, wrap tassel around brad to finish.

•Handy Hint•

Use a hand towel roll for a longer gift box.

Store your glitter in small tubs, so you can easily pop things into it to glitter, and if you have to pour it over the top of an item, it is easier to put back in the pot, than a narrow jar.

This makes a great Easter and Christmas box, just change the colors.

Bunny Pegs

These bunny pegs can be made to suit any occasion, substitute the bunny for a Santa, snowflake or Christmas tree and you will have awesome card pegs for Christmas.

MATERIALS

1 30 x 30 cm (12 x 12 in) cardstock
1 30 x 30 cm (12 x 12 in) chipboard
Wooden pegs
White spray paint
White glitter
Dimensional magic
Purple glitter paper
Any purple patterned paper

Small foam eggs
Twig punch
Doily border punch
Small daisy punch
Pink, yellow and purple liquid pearls
White PVA glue
Tim Holtz Alterations Movers and Shapers bunny
  die
1 pack 3mm pearl strips

STEPS

- Trim the edges off 4 paper plates to form a 12 cm (4.7 in) diameter circle. Adhere 2 plates together, one facing up one facing down. This creates a stable base to adhere the top and bottom to.
- Cut 2 strips of pink cardstock 2 x 30 cm (0.8 x 12 in) and adhere with hot glue gun around the sides of the plates.
- Trim hand towel insert to 14 cm (5.5 in), and cover with patterned paper, punch Doily border from white cardstock and adhere around roll top and bottom, add a second piece to the top a few centimeters (half an inch) below the first one. Trim a 1.5 cm (0.6 in) strip from pink cardstock and adhere to center of roll. Adhere pearls over pink cardstock and doily border as pictured.
- Adhere top and bottom to roll with hot glue.
- Now to decorate, die-cut 3 fences from white cardstock, adhere around the base. Trim a 1 cm (0.4 in) strip from patterned paper and adhere over base of fence, layer over pearl strips.
- Die-cut 8 horses from white cardstock, and also 4 from light weight chipboard. Adhere the white cardstock horse to either side of the chipboard ones.
- Ink edges with pearlescent poppy, apply dimensional magic to surface, smooth out with fingertip and sprinkle with white glitter. Adhere a small pink pearl for an eye. Add a larger pearl to middle of silver trim and carefully adhere small pearls around the edge, repeat 3 more times and adhere to center of each horse.
- Paint 4 straws with gesso, allow to dry, smear with dimensional magic and dip into white glitter. When dry adhere to the back of each horse, trim (save trimmed pieces) and adhere to top of carousel with hot glue. Adhere the base with sticky glue spots.
- Die-cut approximately 20 small banners from patterned papers, ink edges, adhere alternating patterns to the edge of the roof.
- Punch doily border from white cardstock and adhere over banners, layer over medium pearl strip.
- Die-cut 4 pink and 4 yellow party banners (ink edges of pink banners) and adhere around the roof and base of carousel with hot glue gun. Add small paper roses to each join.
- Die-cut 3 of the large kite from pink cardstock and 2 from white cardstock. Die-cut a smaller kite from patterned papers, ink edges. Fold all kites, patterned and plain along the top at the points.
- Snip the patterned kites along that fold and adhere the pieces to the cardstock ones, as pictured.
- Hot glue a piece of straw to the center of the roof, rest all folded kites on an angle so they touch the straw and the sides of the roof, bend the kites so they fit and adhere in place with hot glue. Trim if needed.

- Tuck muslin around edges and wind a little eyelash fiber around the top of the straw.
- Paint a bamboo skewer with gesso, trim a strip of white cardstock to 1 x 10 cm (0.4 x 4 in), ink edges, fold in half and stamp FUN or JOY on both sides, adhere together sandwiching the skewer in between. Trim a V into the one end, smear a little dimensional magic over the flag and dip into a pot of glitter. Insert flag into straw, trimming if needed.
- Die-cut 2 labels, one from pink cardstock and one from white, ink the edges of the white label and stamp a greeting onto the center, adhere to pink label and attach to front of carousel with 3-D foam tape.
- Add pearls to the peaks of the roof and spray with a little silver spray glitter.

•Handy Hint•

Of course you can make this with any patterned papers and any color theme to suit the party or occasion.

I have made a smaller one of these with Christmas colors and it looked lovely, too.

Fill the bottom with sweets or lucky tickets for all of the guests to take.

If you don't have all of the dies, try using found shapes, kites can be hand drawn and a cardboard template made, you can find picket fence chipboard shapes, and there are many rocking or carousel horses die or stamps on the market today.

To add strength pierce a small toothpick through the top of the roof to glue the straw to, fill the straw with hot glue and place over the toothpick.

Christmas Birdie Bon Bon

Bon bons (crackers) are always a must at Christmas time, and this sweet birdie in its nest is sure to become a family favorite.

MATERIALS

1 30 x 30 cm (12 x 12 in) white cardstock

⅓ 30 x 30 cm (12 x 12 in) sheet of Graphic 45 Twelve Days of Christmas collection Joyeux Noel & My True Love patterned paper

⅓ sheet of red and green cardstock

⅓ sheet of brown cardstock

Couture Creations decorations collection bon bon (cracker) die

doily border punch

Spellbinders holly twigs and leaves die

Nested circles die

3mm self-adhesive pearl strips

Fired Brick Distress ink stamp pad

Brown & red glitter

Spray adhesive

Sticky spots

Muslin

Red craft bird

White eyelash fibers

Metallic gold paint

Olive green glimmer mist

White organza ribbon

Red plastic trim

Mouse pad and stylus

Hand die-cutting machine

Hot glue gun

STEPS

- Die-cut the bon bon (cracker) from white cardstock and fold along scored lines, ink edges with red ink and assemble. Tie ends with white organza ribbon.
- Punch 4 strips of border punch from patterned papers, adhere one strip to ends of bon bon. Adhere 2 green strips to center of bon bon.
- Cut a strip of red cardstock 1.5 cm (0.6 in) adhere to center to hide join and trim to fit. Layer over red plastic trim, affixing with hot glue gun.
- Attach pearl strips to ends overlapping red patterned paper.
- Cut lots of strips of brown cardstock, about 3 mm (0.1 in) thick. Scrunch up, unfurl and tuck around each other tying a loose knot. Die-cut a small circle from brown cardstock and hot glue bird nest on top.
- Spray liberally with adhesive and drench with brown glitter. Hot glue to top of bon bon.
- Die-cut holly leaves from green cardstock, use a mouse pad and stylus to add some veins to the leaves and swipe over gold paint. Tuck leaves into each side of the nest, and adhere in place.
- Roll glue spots in your hand until they form a ball, then dip into red glitter, continuing to roll until all red and glittery. Adhere to top of holly leaves.
- Wrap white eyelash fiber around the nest.
- Adhere craft bird to nest, spray a little green glimmer mist onto muslin and tuck beside bird.

•Handy Hint•

These bon bons are made from scraps of paper so are very inexpensive to create.

Fill the center with sweets, small gifts or jewelry.

For a fun thing, type up jokes and rhymes to include into the center of the bon bon.

If you want to pull these apart like regular bon bons, just add a serrated line along the middle.

Christmas Pringle Ornaments

I love Christmas and making small handmade gifts for everybody, this is one of my favorite things to create.

MATERIALS

2 empty Pringle tins

½ sheet 30 x 30 cm (12 x 12 in) Christmas paper

½ sheet Graphic 45 Twelve Days of Christmas, My True love and Drummers Drumming and Ladies Dancing patterned paper

1 A4 sheet of clear acetate

Scalloped and nested circles dies

2 packs of 3mm pearl strips

Red rhinestones

Small Santa & snowman figurine

Mini Christmas trees

Red organza ribbon

Large pearl brad

Bobble bead

Gold and pearl thread

Coarse white glitter

1 tissue

Red glitter washi tape

Red & white glitter

Small hacksaw

Hand die-cutting machine

Hot glue gun

Gesso

Double sided tape

3-D foam tape

Art glitter glue

STEPS

- Cut a large circle from white cardstock approximately 24 cm (9.5 in) in diameter.
- Using a pencil and metal ruler, draw 2 lines to find the center of the circle. Continue until you have dissected the circle into 16ths.
- Die-cut 2 nested circles from patterned paper (the largest being 9.5 cm (3.7 in)) place one in the center of the white circle and trace around it.
- Cut along each pencil line until the patterned circle pencil line to create 16 tabs with a circular base. Fold each tab along the patterned circle line.
- With the stapler, attach each tab to the other, stapling both tabs together. Each tab should overlap each other by about a half, making sure it is at a right angle from the base.
- Adhere the patterned circle to the base, to cover all of the pencil lines.
- Die-cut a scalloped circle from white cardstock and adhere over outside base, layer over patterned circle.
- Punch out 2 borders from white cardstock, adhere one to the inside of the basket. Cover the remaining strip with dimensional magic, smooth out with your fingertip and cover with white glitter. Adhere the outside top of basket with 3-D foam tape.
- Adhere pearl strip over glittered strip.
- Punch out another doily border from white cardstock, flip over and punch out the other side to create a patterned handle.
- Trim out 1 x 30 cm (0.4 x 12 in) strip from patterned paper, adhere to center of handle. Affix pearl strip down the center.
- Attach the handle with a hot glue gun trimming off the excess.
- Adhere eyelash fiber to the top edge of the basket to hide the foam tape.
- Tie a generous bow with organza ribbon and adhere to outside the handle.
- Spray paper rose with spray adhesive and dip into a pot of white glitter, adhere a rose along with 2 daises beside the bow. Tuck pearl sprays, in the cluster of flowers.

•Handy Hint•

You can vary the look of this basket by attaching the tabs looser or tighter.
Make a trial basket first to check out how you would like to attach your tabs.

Elf Boots

Fill these cute elfish boots with sweets, candy canes or a special present for the one you love, they make a wonderful addition to your Christmas table.

MATERIALS

1 30 x 30 cm (12 x 12 in) white cardstock

Graphic 45 Twelve days of Christmas Joyeux Noel and My True Love patterned paper

Couture Creations Extra Loren embossing folder

3mm self-adhesive pearl strips

Large self-adhesive pearls

1/3 strip of red cardstock

White eyelash fibers

Toilet roll insert

Red organza ribbon

2 tiny red bells

Spellbinders holly and twigs dies

nested banner dies

Pearl paint

Gold paint

Hot glue gun

Mouse pad and stylus

Hand die-cutting machine

Double sided tape

3-D foam tape

STEPS

- Trace out door hanger template on to chipboard and patterned paper. Trim out both and adhere together with glue stick. Ink edges.
- Cut a 7 x 14 cm (2.7 x 5.5 in) panel from remaining patterned paper and adhere to chipboard and trim. Ink edges and adhere to door hanger.
- Trim picket fence, paint with gesso, allow to dry and repaint with a thicker layer and dry with heat gun until it blisters and bubbles. Adhere to bottom of door hanger.
- Die-cut a scalloped circle from white cardstock and a matching nested circle from a scrap of patterned paper. Adhere together with 3-D foam tape and attach to top of door hanger.
- Die-cut scalloped heart from white cardstock and a plain heart from red cardstock. Place the scalloped heart on the die-cutting machine plate and die-cut again with a smaller nested heart to make a frame.
- Cover heart frame with dimensional magic, smooth out with your fingertip and sprinkle with white glitter. Allow to dry and adhere over red heart with 3-D foam tape. Adhere to middle of door hanger.
- Cut a rosette from apricot cardstock, fold up and adhere the ends together, squash and adhere in shape with hot glue gun. Brush edges with dimensional magic and dip into a pot of white glitter. Adhere over top of large scalloped heart. Wrap white eyelash fiber around edges. Affix buttons, red pearl and resin heart as pictured.
- Dab black ink all over alphabet chipboard, cover with dimensional magic and dip into black glitter, affix to center of heart.
- Paint girl silhouettes with gesso and allow to dry, spray with dylusions, dry with heat gun and cover with dimensional magic, smooth out with your fingertip, and sprinkle with a tiny bit of white glitter.
- Adhere to bottom of hanger. To finish, snip pearl strips into 2 pearls and adhere with glue around the edge of the heart.

•Handy Hint•

Add your own personal bits and pieces, you can use any color buttons pearls and shapes.
By snipping the pearl strips into pieces you can easily make the strip go around curves
and shapes, it is a little time consuming but results in such a nice effect.
Make these door hangers in any theme; Christmas, Mother's Day, Easter and even
Halloween for a fun decoration in your home.

Frosty Snow Globe

This is one of my favorite things to make at Christmas, anyone who receives this will treasure it forever.

MATERIALS

Plastic bauble

½ sheet of 30 x 30 cm (12 x 12 in) teal cardstock

½ sheet of 30 x 30 cm (12 x 12 in) white cardstock

½ sheet of 30 x 30 cm (12 x 12 in) chipboard

Diamond dust

Couture Creations fir tree dies

Tim Holtz mover and shapers deer die

Assorted snowflake punches

Fence border punch

Couture Creations Extra Loren embossing folder

Walnut stain Distress stain

Liquid pearls

Pearl paint

3mm self-adhesive pearl strips

Gesso

White glitter

Ocean Depth Dew Drops stamp pad

White eyelash fiber

Spray adhesive

Turquoise glimmer mists

3 large self-adhesive pearl

Small alphabet stamps

Dimensional magic

Art glitter glue

Scalloped & Nested circle dies

Hot glue gun

Hand die-cutting machine

Double sided tape

3-D foam tape

STEPS

- Paint the edges of plastic bauble with gesso, allow to dry, smear over dimensional magic with fingertip and sprinkle with white glitter, set aside to dry.
- Using template cut out base of snow globe from teal cardstock, emboss with folder. Dry brush raised areas with pearl paint, and adhere ends together.
- Die-cut scalloped circle from white cardstock, apply dimensional magic over edges, and sprinkle with white glitter. Allow to dry, then adhere to base.
- Punch fence border from white cardstock, attach to base with hot glue, layer over a pearl strip.
- Die-cut a plain circle that will fit nicely into bauble, also die-cut 4 trees with fir tree die. Adhere 2 trees back to back, spritz with a small amount of turquoise, allow to dry. Apply dimensional magic to trees, smooth over with your fingertip and sprinkle with white glitter, repeat for both sides.
- Scrunch up a small torn piece of white cardstock, spray with adhesive and drench with white glitter. Affix scrunched paper over top of plain circle, to create a snowy hill and affix trees with hot glue trimming one if needed.
- Die-cut small deer from chipboard, dab distress stain over front and back of deer. Allow to dry, and once dry, coat both sides with dimensional magic. When dry add small dots of liquid pearls as the eye and dots on the rump.
- Adhere beside trees with hot glue, trimming the feet if needed.
- Mix 1 teaspoon of diamond dust with ½ teaspoon of gesso and a few drops of dimensional magic in a small container, to make faux snow. Layer around edges and over the scrunched paper until you are happy with the look.
- Affix the finished scene into one half of the bauble, secure in place with hot glue and snap on other half of bauble.
- Apply a strip of pearls around the bauble join. Attach bauble to base, with hot glue and add a line Art Glitter glue to seal. Wrap white eyelash fibers around the join.
- Punch a large snowflake and 2 smaller ones from white cardstock, cover with dimensional magic and sprinkle with white glitter, add pearl to centers of snowflakes and adhere to front of bauble.
- Trim out a strip of white cardstock, scrunch and unfurl, stamp with a Christmas greeting, ink edges with Ocean Depth ink. Trim and create a scroll adhere at 2 points to the sides of the bauble.

Halloween Pringle Lumieres

Add some Halloween spookiness with this recycled pringle tin candle lumieres, they are so inexpensive and easy you will want to make lots of them!

MATERIALS

Small pringle tins

Flat black spray paint

Scalpel

½ 30 x 30 cm (12 x 12 in) sheet of black & orange cardstock

½ 30 x 30 cm (12 x 12 in) sheet of Halloween patterned paper

½ 30 x 30 cm (12 x 12 in) sheet of plain vellum

Orange glitter

White glitter

Black glitter

Purple glitter

Small rosette die

Scalloped and nested circle dies

Doily and double arches border punch

Jack-o'-lantern punch

Cuttlebug cut and emboss creepy bats and spider die

Jet black archival ink stamp pad

Black eyelash fiber

Small skull beads

Bat buttons

½ inch circle punch

Black enamel dots

Black rhinestones

3 mm self-adhesive pearl strips

Hand die-cutting machine

Hot glue gun

Double sided tape

3-D foam tape

STEPS

- Cut a circle from the center of an old pringle tin and cut 4 vertical panels from a second tin. Spray both tins with black spray paint and allow to dry.
- To decorate the circle tin, adhere a small panel of vellum to the inside of the tin.
- Punch out Double arches border from orange cardstock and adhere to top and bottom of tin.
- Paint 2 strips of pearls with black spray paint, allow to dry, then peel off and apply over orange border.
- Die-cut a medium scalloped circle from orange cardstock, re-cut scalloped circle with a nested circle to create a frame. Apply dimensional magic over the surface, smooth out with fingertip and sprinkle with orange glitter. When dry, adhere over window with 3-D foam tape. Adhere black rhinestones around frame.
- Die-cut small rosette from orange cardstock, adhere ends together, squash into shape and hot glue into a rosette. Dry brush dimensional magic around the edges and dip into a pot of white glitter. Adhere to side of window. Wrap black fibers around the rosette.
- Die-cut 3 bats from black cardstock, apply dimensional magic over surface, smooth out with fingertip and cover with black glitter, allow to dry. Adhere to top of rosette and around the frame.
- Punch a small circle from black cardstock and adhere to rosette, adhere a small skull bead over top. Smear dimensional magic over rim of tin, dip into orange glitter.
- To decorate second tin, adhere strips of vellum inside tin. Punch Doily border from patterned paper. Adhere to top and bottom of tin.
- Cut two 6mm strips from patterned paper, apply dimensional magic over entire strip, smooth out with your fingertip and sprinkle with purple glitter. Adhere to top and bottom with double sided tape.
- Die-cut a scalloped circle and punch 4 pumpkins from orange cardstock, cover with dimensional magic and sprinkle with orange glitter. Adhere scalloped circle to front of tin, with 3-D foam tape. Die-cut a small circle from patterned paper and affix over top with 3-D foam tape. Wrap with black eyelash fiber.
- Decorate with bat button, glittered pumpkin, black enamel dot and a 'Trick or Treat' tag cut from patterned paper.
- Adhere remaining pumpkins around the sides of tin. Cover rim with dimensional magic and dip into black glitter to finish.

•Handy Hint•

Use your die as a guide to cut out the window in the tin, die-cut a scrap and hold down while you trace around it with a pen.

You could also turn these into sweet tins, just add a handle.

Change the colors and they would be awesome Christmas candle holders.

Add extra glue to rhinestones to make them adhere better.

Hanging Heart Token

You can whip up this elegant heart token in no time at all. It makes a lovely wedding token or Valentines gift.

MATERIALS

1 30 x 30 cm (12 x 12 in) sheets of chipboard

A4 white pearl Tuscany embossed paper

1 scrap of pink patterned paper

1 large paper rose

3 medium paper roses

3 white medium paper roses

4 small paper roses

2 packs 3mm pearl self-adhesive strips

Medium 5mm self-adhesive pearl strips

1 resin rose

White pearl paint

White organza ribbon

Scalloped and nested circles dies

White glitter

Dimensional magic

Spray adhesive

Large Heart 3-Die

Crop-a-dile hand punch

Double sided tape

3-D foam tape.

Hot glue gun

Hand die-cutting machine

STEPS

- Die-cut heart from chipboard with heart die. Also die-cut embossed paper twice.
- Adhere embossed paper to both sides of chipboard heart.
- Punch a hole in the top of the heart with Crop-a-dile hand punch thread through ribbon and tie off in a knot.
- Spray the large and medium paper roses with spray adhesive and dip into a pot of white glitter, when dry cluster with the smaller roses into the center of the heart.
- Snip up medium pearl strip and adhere around the edges of the heart, with glue.
- Flip over, die-cut a small circle from patterned paper and adhere to the center of the heart.
- Die-cut a larger scalloped circle from white cardstock, roll through machine again with a nested circle to create a small scalloped frame. Cover with Dimensional magic, smooth out with your fingertip and dip into a pot of white glitter.
- Adhere glittered frame over patterned circle with 3-D foam tape.
- Paint resin rose with pearl paint adhere to center of frame.
- Snip small pearl strip into 2 pearls and adhere around the edge of the heart with glue.
- Tie a generous bow with organza ribbon and affix to top of heart with hot glue gun.

•Handy Hint•

Apply pearl paint to the edges of the heart to hide the chipboard and make it look neater.

You can trace around a template create the heart chipboard shape, or hand draw them for a folksy look.

You can make this in pinks and reds for a wonderful Valentines token.

This makes a heartfelt gift for a bride to carry down the aisle on her arm.

Heart Token Box

This gorgeous heart shaped box is not just for Valentine's day, it also makes a lovely gift box for small items, such as jewellery.

MATERIALS

1 30 x 30 cm (12 x 12 in) white sheet

⅓ 30 x 30 cm (12 x 12 in) sheet of green cardstock

1 30 x 30 cm (12 x 12 in) sheet of Couture Creations vintage rose rouge damask patterned paper

Pearlescent poppy dew drop stamp pad

3mm adhesive pearl strips

White eyelash fiber

2 paper medium roses

Pearl sprays

White glitter

Spray adhesive

Dimensional magic

Imaginarium chipboard word (LOVE)

Peeled paint distress ink

Finger stall

Embossing stamp pad

Utee (Ultra thick Embossing Enamel)

White and black dylusions

Gold embossing powder

Doily border punch

Small white bow or ribbon to make one

½ metre cream organza ribbon

Double sided tape and foam tape squares

Scalloped and nested hearts dies

Scalloped and nested circles dies

Foliage dies

Hand die-cutting machine

Hot glue gun and heat gun

Bamboo skewer

Wet wipes

STEPS

- Cut 2 Scalloped hearts from white cardstock and 3 plain hearts from patterned paper, ink edges.
- Adhere 2 of the patterned hearts to one White scallop heart leaving 2 spots unglued on either side of one of the hearts. This will be for the ribbon and hinge.
- Place heart on die-cutting machine plate, layer over a small circle die to cut out the middle (keep circle).
- Trim organza ribbon in half and tuck into one of the sides of the heart, hot glue to secure in place. Cut a small piece of scrap white cardstock into a 4 x 3 cm (1.5 x 2 in) tab, fold in half and insert into other side of heart.
- Adhere remaining patterned heart to second white scallop heart, leave a small section un-glued to tuck in the other half of the ribbon.
- Cut a strip of white cardstock 7 x 30 cm (3 x 12 in), score at 2.5 and 5 cm (1 and 2 in) along the 7 cm (3 in) side, fold along scores. Snip small tabs all along bottom of 2 cm (0.8 in) fold. Adhere the 2.5 cm (1 in) score over top to line up with 5 cm (2 in) score. This will create a double cardstock edge with a snipped tab border.
- Adhere tape all over white scalloped heart back, making sure no tape shows on the very edges.
- Line up both ends of white strip to point of heart and affix down, (no need to overlap) then gently bend the sides to form a heart shape over the tape. Secure with hot glue if needed.
- Cut a slit in the top of white strip, to line up with the tab on the lid. Insert the white cardstock tab and hot glue to secure.
- Trim 2.3 cm (0.9 in) strip of patterned paper, ink edges and adhere to side of heart box.
- Punch white cardstock with Doily punch, trim to fit inside box and adhere in place, cut another thin strip of patterned paper to adhere to the bottom of the Doily lace strip.
- Cut 2 Scalloped circles from white cardstock, re die-cut with plain circle to create 2 circular scalloped frames. Apply a coat of Dimensional magic, smooth out with your finger and sprinkle with white glitter. Adhere one to front of box with 3-D foam tape and the other to inside of box. Wrap fibers around front circular frame.
- Wrap wire stems of paper roses around a bamboo skewer. Spray paper roses with adhesive and dip into a tub of white glitter, allow to dry and adhere to middle of heart box, over top of circular frame.
- Die-cut leaves from green cardstock, use finger stall to daub over Peeled paint ink. Spritz with a little white dylusions and dry. Cover leaves with embossing ink and sprinkle over UTEE, heat to melt with heat gun and while still hot spritz with a little white dylusions, continue to heat for a few seconds to dry.

- Tuck leaves under roses along with pearl sprays and use hot glue to secure in place.
- Using the base of the box as a template, cut out a white cardstock heart to fit inside bottom, trim to fit. Fussy cut flowers from patterned paper and adhere to base of box with 3-D foam tape and trim off excess.
- Ink the cardstock circle saved from earlier and adhere with 3-D foam tape to center of box, wrap fibers around it.
- Emboss chip word with gold embossing powder, allow to cool, then spray with black dylusions and wipe off excess with a wet wipe. Adhere to middle of raised circle. Add a green dew drop and white bow as pictured.

•Handy Hint•

Pearl sprays can be found at wedding shops.

A bamboo skewer can help you with wrapping eyelash fibers and holding glued items in place.

You could add a photo to the base of the box, instead of the flowers and chipboard word.

Hoppy Birthday Explosion box

Here is one for the froggy lovers out there, of course if you are not so fond of frogs, change it to another animal to make a sweet surprise explosion box.

MATERIALS

1 30 x 30 cm (12 x 12 in) sheet olive green cardstock

1 30 x 30 cm (12 x 12 in) sheet of white cardstock

1 15 x 15 cm (6 x 6 in) yellow cardstock

1 inch circle and sun (small & large) punch

Ultimate Crafts Celosia Collection Daffodil die

Ultimate Crafts Celosia Collection Crystal flake die

Squares

Twig punch

Any embossing folder

Black eyelash fiber

Dimensional magic

Large yellow gemstone

2 smaller yellow rhinestones

Cut grass, white linen and black marble ranger
   dylusions spray ink

Night sky dew drop ink stamp pad

Jet black archival stamp pad

Inka Gold blue rub on metallic paint

Birthday greeting stamp

Plastic green frog

Silver spray glitter

Hot glue gun

Heat gun

Hand die-cutting machine

Double sided tape

3-D foam tape squares

Mouse pad and stylus

Bamboo skewer

Gesso

STEPS

- Trace around template onto olive green cardstock and trim out. Score on fold lines and assemble box.
- Die-cut 5 medium squares and 3 smaller medium squares with nesting dies and white cardstock, emboss with embossing folder, then spray with cut grass dylusions, dry with heat gun. Rub night sky ink over raised areas and edges, rub over metallic blue paint, flick white linen dylusions over squares and dry with heat gun. Adhere to all 5 larger squares of the box bottom.
- Die-cut 6 of the crystal flake with white cardstock, place on a mouse pad and cup apply pressure over the surface with the stylus to cup the die-cut. Adhere 3 layered over each other counter setting the petals.
- Punch out 6 of the small sun punch from yellow cardstock, layer 3 over each other on the center of the white flower. Add a small yellow rhinestone and adhere to 2 of the side panels.
- Punch out 4 or 5 leaves, from olive cardstock, apply a little white linen over the leaves with your fingertip. Adhere to top central square.
- Punch 3 circles from olive cardstock, trim out a small section to resemble a lily pad, place on mouse pad and score veins in leaf. Ink with night sky stamp pad and cover entire leaf with dimensional magic. When dry adhere to central square with 3-D foam tape.
- Dab green frog with a little gesso, allow to dry and spray with cut grass dylusions, when dry spray with silver glitter glue. Place on lily pads.
- Adhere the 2 smaller squares to the lid and inside lid of the box, using 3-D foam tape. Wrap black fiber around the top lid.
- Die-cut 3-Daffodil dies from white cardstock, use mouse pad to shape them. Adhere layering them over each other and counter setting the petals.
- Punch out 3 of the large sun from yellow cardstock, shape with mouse pad and stylus, adhere to center of flower, add a large yellow gemstone.
- Trim the third smaller square into 4 strips and adhere around the edges of the lid top.
- Stamp birthday greeting onto a scrap of white cardstock, trim, ink edges and attach to inside lid with 3-D foam tape.

Jack in the Box

Try making this interactive Jack and the Box in darker colors for a grungier look.

MATERIALS

Cocoa Vanilla Sugar N Spice Collection, Journal Cards, Garden Girl, and Perfect Posies patterned paper

2 30 x 30 cm (12 x 12 in) sheet teal cardstock

½ 30 x 30 cm (12 x 12 in) sheet pink cardstock

1 30 x 30 cm (12 x 12 in) sheet white cardstock

2 packs 3mm pearl strips

1 pack white self-adhesive pearls

2 pink & blue paper cherry blossom flowers

1 large white paper rose

Pink braid, white eyelash fibers

2 plastic goggle eyes

1 small white tassel

Nested circles

Couture Creations Everyday Essentials strawberry leaf die

Couture Creations Everyday Essentials Twisting corners die

Nested and scalloped squares

Scalloped and nested oval dies.

Small rosette die

Spray adhesive

Calypso teal ranger dylusions

White glitter

Doily border punch

Small white bow

Pearlescent poppy dew drops ink

Dimensional magic

Sun and daisy punch

Green metallic paint

White brads

- Trace out templates onto teal cardstock and cut out.
- Adhere together to form a box, with one side flipping down and lid.
- Die-cut 4 large squares from pink cardstock and adhere to outside of box bottom.
- Die-cut 4 smaller squares from patterned papers and adhere over pink cardstock ones.
- Die-cut 5 large squares from patterned papers, adhere to inside of box and box lid.
- Die-cut 2 large squares from white cardstock and adhere to bottom of box and the top of lid.
- Cut a strip from patterned paper 2 cm (0.8 in) wide, and adhere around the edge of box top. Punch out doily border punch from white cardstock and adhere to the bottom edge of lid, layer over pearl strips and pink trim. Insert white brad to front and wrap around a small tassel.
- Die-cut a scalloped square from patterned paper and adhere over white square on lid with 3-D foam tape. Wrap around white fibers, affix medium pearls to each corner.
- Die-cut a journal card into a circle and adhere to top of lid with 3-D foam tape.
- Die-cut 2 leaves from a scrap of green cardstock, brush over green metallic paint and adhere to top when dry.
- Spritz white paper rose with water. Spritz an acetate sheet with teal dylusions to form a small puddle. Dip edges of petals into the puddle. Allow color to wick up the petals, dry with heat gun. Spray with adhesive and dip into white glitter. Adhere over leaves and affix small pearls as pictured.
- Cut another journal card and adhere to inside of lid with 3-D foam tape, decorate with trimmed tags. Punch out white daisies and tuck under tags.
- Die-cut twisted corners from teal cardstock, adhere to inside white square.
- Trim 2 strips of white cardstock 4 cm (1.6 in)wide, and 2 patterned strips, adhere both strips together, adhere white strip at right angle to patterned strip and fold over concertina fashion. Secure ends and fold upwards. Adhere to center of box.
- Cut 2 circles from pink cardstock, and adhere to either side of folded up section. Wrap white fibers around the edges, attach with glue.
- Die-cut rosette from white cardstock, fold up, adhere ends together and assemble with hot glue, brush edges with Dimensional magic and sprinkle with white glitter. Snip in half and adhere either side of head. Add more hot glue if the rosette unfurls. Affix a small bow at the throat.
- Punch out the sun from a scrap of black card, snip into quarters and adhere two quarters to either side of head. Layer over goggle eyes, add white brad for a nose and draw in a mouth. Brush a little pearlescent poppy to either side for the cheeks.
- Die-cut a journal tag and adhere to fold down flap on the inside.

- Die-cut scalloped oval from white cardstock and a plain oval from a journal card. Adhere one over the other with 3-D foam tape. Attach to front of box.

•Handy Hint•

Curl wire ends of paper flowers around a bamboo skewer to create a nice coiled tendril.

Cover the back of the splayed brads with a small circle of blue cardstock for a neat appearance.

This box looks great made in black cardstock, with vintage circus or clown papers as decoration.

Magic Carousel Mini Book

Create this fold up Carousel in any color as a beautiful keepsake for any new Mother. After it has served as a decoration it can be folded up and put away for baby in the future.

MATERIALS

2 sheets 30 x 30 cm (12 x 12 in) cardstock

1 15 x 15 cm (6 x 6 in) white and green cardstock

White copy paper

Graphic 45 Once Upon a Springtime Fairy Folk & Primrose Cottage patterned paper

2 packs 3mm self-adhesive pearl strips

white self-adhesive pearls

White glitter

Ocean depth dew drops stamp pad

Dimensional magic

2 border punch

Doily border punch

Carousel horse punch

Small daisy punch

Yellow stamp pad

Jet black archival ink

Clear embossing powder

Yellow glitter glue

2 medium paper roses

Twig punch

Bamboo skewer

Mini alphabet stamps

Nested Squares dies

Nested Rectangle dies

Sentiments Clear stamp set

Hand die-cutting machine

50 cm (20 in) Pink and blue organza ribbon

Hot glue gun

Heat gun

Double sided tape

3-D foam tape squares

Spray adhesive

STEPS

- Trace template 6 times onto blue cardstock and cut out. Fold in half and place carefully on plate of die-cutting machine and line up a medium square die approximately 1 cm (0.4 in) away from the side and bottom edge, roll through machine cutting both sides at one. Do this to 4 of the panels.
- For the remaining 2 panels cut the nested square from one side only, one on the right and the other on the left.
- Cut six small strips of cardstock 10 x 0.5 cm (4 x 0.2 in), adhere these to the middle of each window, vertically.
- Punch out 12 carousel horses, apply dimensional magic to each horse and smooth out with your fingertip. Sprinkle with white glitter. Make sure 6 horses face to the left and 6 to the right.
- Adhere each horse the center strip, placing a left and right one over top of each other sandwiching the pole in between.
- Apply double sided tape to the sides, bottom and folded edge of every second panel. Adhere together, leaving the top sloping section unglued.
- Punch a doily punch from copy paper, attach to the bottom of each panel. Cut a 1.2 cm (0.5 in) strip from patterned paper and layer over top of white copy paper.
- Cut six roof panels using the template, score in the middle and fold in half, fold and score tabs as well. The center fold should be a valley fold and the tabs are both mountain folds.
- Punch out border punch from blue cardstock and adhere to the edges of each roof panel. Allow an extra 2 cm to hang over each side tab. Apply tape to each tab on both sides. Peel off tape from one side and adhere to cover, then peel the second tab and insert into the top of the roof panels. This is a tricky part as you must slot the next roof panel in before pressing down to adhere.
- Trim and tuck the blue cardstock trim into each roof panel join, use hot glue to secure if needed. Affix pearl strips to join and snip at the fold, so the strips don't scrunch up when the book is folded.
- Paint a bamboo skewer white, and dip into glitter. Trim a 1 x 10 cm (0.4 x 4 in) strip from white cardstock, fold in half and stamp JOY onto each side. Remove tape and sandwich around bamboo skewer. Snip a large V on one end and slide into one of the roof panels, securing in place with hot glue.
- Use template to cut 2 covers from patterned paper, trim to fit, ink edges and adhere to the front and back cover with double sided tape. Adhere more paper lace and strip of patterned paper to the bottom of covers. Layer ribbons over covers and around spine.
- Die-cut 2 rectangles from blue cardstock, ink edges and attach to front covers, over ribbons.

- Stamp greetings onto white cardstock with black ink, sprinkle over with clear embossing powder and heat set. Die-cut with a smaller rectangle, ink edges with yellow ink and adhere to front covers with 3-D foam tape. Affix small pearls to each corner of blue panel.
- Fussy cut 2 images from patterned paper. Adhere to covers with 3-D foam tape.
- Spray adhesive all over paper roses and dip into a pot of glitter, when dry adhere to covers. Punch out 4 leaves from green cardstock and tuck either side of roses.
- Punch 6 daisies from white cardstock and adhere around the covers. Add a small dot of yellow stickles to the centers and allow to dry.

•Handy Hint•

The roof panels may need extra strong glue or hot glue to adhere together.

Take care when lining up the spine, don't worry about the windows, they can be easily trimmed to match.

You can other shapes than a carousel horse, consider a ballerina, dragon, flowers, little tags, images cut from decorator paper.

Use a mouse pad and stylus to shape the fussy cut images and white daisies.

Stamp the year of the baby on the flag for a personalized addition.

Mini Two-tier Cake

Make a gorgeous tiered cake that looks good enough to eat, just fill with sweets and give to a lucky friend.

MATERIALS

2 small nested paper mache boxes

1 30 x 30 cm (12 x 12 in) of white cardstock

1 15 x 15 cm (6 x 6 in) piece of green cardstock

2 packs 3mm pearl adhesive strips

Doily border punch

1 A4 sheet of pearl patterned paper

White glitter

Dimensional magic

Paper doily or doily die

Large self-adhesive pearls

White pony beads

White pearl paint

White eyelash fibers

Thin white satin ribbon

3 large pink paper roses

3 pink heart pins

Foliage die

Nested circle die

Peeled paint distress ink stamp pad

Worn lipstick distress ink stamp pad

Mouse pad and stylus

Blending foam

White matt spray paint

Hand die-cutting machine

Double sided tape

3-D foam tape

Hot glue gun

STEPS

- Spray paint inside and out both small boxes.
- Trim the striped paper to fit the outside bottom of the boxes and adhere in place.
- Cut circle to fit lids of boxes from white cardstock. Cover circles with Dimensional magic and smooth out with your fingertip. Sprinkle with white glitter and when dry attach to top of cakes.
- Punch doily border from white cardstock, adhere around the top of the box lid.
- Adhere white satin ribbon over top and layer over pearl strips.
- Rub pearl paint over a paper doily and attach larger box at the bottom.
- Adhere large pearls to white pony beads with glue and arrange around the edge of the lid of larger box,
- Add a pearl strip to bottom of small box, and adhere 3 paper roses to the middle of the lid. Wrap around white fibers, and insert heart pins.
- Die-cut leaves from green cardstock with Spellbinders die. Flip over on mouse pad and score in leaf veins.
- Flip back over and blend peeled paint over leaves, then blend a little worn lipstick over the tips. Snip up leaves and tuck around roses.

•Handy Hint•

You can make this in any color for any celebration.

If you don't have a circle die that fits your boxes, just use the lids as a template and hand cut out carefully.

Mini Cupcake Chocolate Box

This tiny cupcake box is an elegant addition to any wedding table, fill with a decadent chocolate to thank all of your guests.

MATERIALS

1 30 x 30 cm (12 x 12 in) of white cardstock

1 10 x 10 cm (4 x 4 in) green cardstock

Couture Creations Lovingly baroque embossing folder

Leaf punch

Small red paper rose

Spray adhesive

White glitter

Pearlescent poppy dew drop stamp pad ink

White eyelash fiber

Pearl paint

Small greeting stamp

Jet Black Archival stamp pad

Hot glue gun

Hand die-cutting machine

Double sided tape

- Trace out both templates onto cream cardstock and trim out. Score along all fold lines. Adhere both pieces to form a box. The base will measure 9 x 9 cm and the top flaps will be 7 x 9 cm (3 x 3.5 in).
- Cut the score lines in between the rectangular panels, stopping at the 9 x 9cm (3.5 x 3.5 in) panels. This will form the flip down sides as pictured.
- From the excess cardstock, cut 3 small panels 13 x 4 cm (5 x 1.5 in), score at each end to create a 2 cm (0.8 in) tab, fold one mountain and one valley to form a Z shape. Adhere to middle of box, spacing evenly from the front. Make sure to keep the 9 cm (3.5 in) section of the panel straight.
- Die-cut baby's breath paper 4 times with square die, ink edges and adhere to outside square sides.
- Die-cut baby's breath paper 4 times with rectangle die, ink edges. Matt onto peach rectangles 7.5 x 6cm (3 x 2 in) and adhere to rectangular flaps, on the top.
- Punch 3 strips of doily lace from cream cardstock, adhere to bottom square sides of box, make sure you trim them to fit each side. Do not adhere around the fold, as this will stop the box folding down. Adhere a second strip on top of the other. Cut a 6 mm (0.2 in) strip of patterned paper and adhere over the paper lace join. Add pearl trip to 3 sides and the fourth side leave a little gap in the pearls for the rosette later.
- Cut another 6 mm (0.2 in) strip of patterned paper and adhere to the 2 side panels only. Fussy cut 2 postage stamps and adhere with 3-D foam tape. Affix pearl strips to the patterned paper strips visible beside the postage stamps.
- Die-cut a scalloped oval from white cardstock, apply dimensional magic, spread out with your fingertip and sprinkle with white glitter. Adhere to front flap. Trim Cherish from patterned paper and adhere with 3-D foam tape over top of oval. Attach seam binding bow, small rose and punched leaves either side.
- Trim out a panel from Cutie pie paper, and adhere to top panel, (stamp MUM/MOM now)
- Die-cut 2 rosettes from cream cardstock adhere at each end, squash together to form a rosette and secure in place with hot glue. Brush edges with dimensional magic and dip into white glitter.
- Add a large pearl to large rosette and smaller pearl to small one. Adhere the small one to the top over cutie pie panel and the larger one to the front of box, in the space left in the pearl strips.
- Trim postage stamp with scalloped scissors and tuck beside small rosette. Add 3 flowers and a punched leaf. Insert the 2 heart pins, into the rosette. Trim out So Sweet panel from patterned paper and affix with 3-D foam tape to the top cutie pie oval panel.
- Fussy cut remaining images from cuddle time and cutie pie, adhere to panels inside box, trim as need. You may need to attach images temporarily to check the position is right and then adhere

down securely, when you are a sure they can all be seen nicely. Tuck teased muslin in the images and secure with a small amount of glue.

- Spray lightly with silver spray glitter, over images and top oval panel.
- Use a small stiff bristle brush to dry brush Pearlescent poppy to the centers of the paper flowers, make sure there is very little ink on the brush to give a soft look.

•Handy Hint•

Print out template onto white paper and adhere to thick cardboard and trim out, to create a sturdy template to use over and over again.

If the top panel flops down too much, insert a toothpick into the back, tucking into the patterned paper panel. This will strengthen the score line.

You could adapt any Graphic 45 paper, to suit this box, and make them in various themes.

Owl Treat Box

This cute little owl is great as a Halloween treat box. You can also jazz it up with red and green for a Christmas box.

MATERIALS

1 30 x 30 cm (12 x 12 in) sheet of white cardstock

½ 30 x 30 cm (12 x 12 in) sheet of teal cardstock

1 10 x 10 cm (4 x 4 in) piece of green cardstock

1/3 1 30 x 30 cm (12 x 12 in) sheet of brown cardstock

Gingerbread dew drops stamp pad

Ocean depth dew drops stamp pad

Sun punch

Scalloped border punch

1.2 and 2.5 cm (1and ½ in) punch

Feather die

Twig punch

2 small pine cones

White eyelash fibers

2 large yellow plastic gems

String

2 white brads

White glitter

Dimensional magic

Stylus and mouse pad

Toilet roll insert

Embossing folder

Nested ovals die

Scalloped Circles die

1/16 hand hole punch

Hand die-cutting machine

Hot glue gun

Double sided tape

3-D foam tape

Silver spray glitter

Quilling tool

STEPS

- Trim center of toilet roll to approximately 6 cm (2.3 in), cut white cardstock to 6 x 12 cm (2.3 x 5 in) and emboss with folder and brush ocean depth ink over the raised areas. Adhere around outside of toilet roll and trim off excess.
- Die-cut a scalloped circle from white cardstock and adhere to bottom of toilet roll.
- Die-cut 2 of the large oval from teal cardstock, ink edges in gingerbread ink, adhere to both sides of base, squashing the base a little.
- With scalloped punch, cut 8 strips approximately 10 cm (4 in) long, ink edges with ocean depth and adhere overlapping each other to the front oval. No need to cover the top 2 cm (0.8 in).
- Use the hole punch to insert two holes in both the front and back, tie together with string.
- Trace around template for owl face, trim out and ink with gingerbread ink. Use a mouse pad and stylus to shape the face a little.
- Punch out sun shape in white cardstock, and circle punches in teal and brown. Snip sun shape in half, ink edges and adhere either side of face. Layer over circle shapes.
- Cut four 0.5 cm (0.2 in) strips from brown cardstock, with a quilling tool roll up the strips, adhering 2 on the one roll, remove from tool and use hot glue to secure.
- Adhere to owl eyes, and add large yellow gemstones. Cut out a small triangle from teal cardstock, cover with dimensional magic and sprinkle with glitter. When dry affix in between eyes as a beak.
- Wrap white fibers around the head of the owl.
- Die-cut 6 feathers, flip over on a mouse pad and score lines over the feathers. Flip back, and ink the top with ocean depth and the bottom with gingerbread ink. Trim to fit the owl box, layer 3 over each other and punch a hole, insert a white brad into all three to hold together, and through the back of the box.
- Die-cut a smaller white oval, adhere to the back of the box, to cover the brad legs. Cut a small triangle into the bottom of the oval.
- Punch out 2 twigs from green cardstock, adhere along with 2 small pinecones to the bottom of the box.
- Lightly spray the back and some of the front with silver glitter spray.

•Handy Hint•

If you don't have a feather die, use 3 long oval shapes as the wings instead.

Use a hand towel roll if you are concerned about hygiene or wrap anything that you place in the treat box.

Create these boxes in a variety of colors and mix up how you arrange the face for completely different owlish looks.

Consider adding small real feathers to the bottom of the box for a touch of nature.

Potent Potion Book

With a few found items, you can make this creepy potion book. Add teas and scents to the bottles for a fun scented décor piece

MATERIALS

1 30 x 30 cm (12 x 12 in) sheet of black cardstock

1 30 x 30 cm (12 x 12 in) sheet of chipboard

1 sheet of Graphic 45 Olde Curiosity Shoppe
  Collection Bazaar of Wonders patterned paper

3 pages of old book paper

2 lids of paper mache square boxes

1 toilet roll insert

4 medium sized glass vials

3 small sized glass vials

3 packs 3mm self-adhesive pearl strips

1 pack large self-adhesive pearls

2 mm (0.08 in) red self-adhesive gemstones

Sticky spots

1 large enamel dot

Gold glitter

Resin flower

Dimensional magic

Black spray paint

Black braid trim

Black eyelash fiber

Gold organza ribbon

Metallic gold paint

8 metal corner trinkets

1 metal square trinkets

Prima trinket

Plastic lizards

Feather

green glitter, crushed

Gold trim

Couture Creations Amaryllis Simone's style die

Small chipboard alphabet

Scalloped die

Nested circle die

Cuttlebug cut and emboss creepy bat and spider
  die

Cherish Me Atherton A4 embossing folder

Glue stick

Hot glue gun

Hand die-cutting machine

Black nikko pen

STEPS

- Spray paint box lids and toilet roll with black spray paint.
- Cut two panels from chipboard 11.5 x 11.5 cm (4.5 x 4.5 in) or a little larger than the lids.
- Emboss black cardstock with A4 embossing folder, trim into 2 pieces adhere to covers with glue stick, fold over edges and trim the corners, adhere down sides with double sided tape. Dry brush raised areas and edges with gold paint.
- Adhere panels to top of lids with hot glue. Make sure one side is flush with the box lid. Cut 6 fine strips approximately 3 mm x 30 cm (0.1 x 12 in), adhere to sides of the lids, apply gold paint with your fingertip. When dry draw over with black pen.
- Cut toilet roll into a 3 x 4 cm (1 x 1.5 in) curve, adhere to each cover, tucking in where the lids meet the chipboard panel flush. Trim gold braid and adhere to top and bottom of spine, also affix gold ribbon to middle of spine.
- Trim 2 panels of chipboard and of black cardstock 9 x 9 cm (3.5 x 3.5 in), adhere black cardstock card to tops of chipboard, dry brush with gold paint. Adhere to front and back of book sandwiching gold ribbon underneath.
- Adhere corner trinkets to the corners of each of the panel's, front and back, adhere square trinket and enamel dot, to the back panel only. Layer over pearls using a little extra glue to form a secure bond.
- Die-cut medium scalloped circle from a scrap of cream cardstock, recut with a nested circle to create a frame. Apply dimensional magic over top and smooth out with your fingertip, dip into a pot of gold glitter.
- Die-cut book papers with a medium nested circle, adhere to center of front cover, affix glittered frame over top with 3-D foam tape, and wrap with black fibers.
- Fussy cut butterfly, coat with dimensional magic and adhere to center of frame. Add in resin flower and trimmed out tag. Carefully adhere chip letters below the tag.
- Cover the inside spine with a small strip of black cardstock, allow for the book to open, do not glue too tightly.
- Trim book papers to cover the inside of the book and adhere in place with glue stick.
- Cut out 2 panels from patterned papers, ink edges and affix inside with 3-D foam tape.
- Die-cut bat from black cardstock, apply dimensional magic over top, smooth out with fingertip, and dip into a pot of black glitter. Add small red 2 mm (0.8 in) gemstones for eyes, adhere to inside top left hand side.

- Fussy cut 2 more butterflies and add to right hand side along with prima trinket. Adhere pearl strip and black trim underneath butterflies.
- Fill bottles, and adhere to inside book. I have filled mine with small plastic lizards, tea leaves, a fussy cut butterfly, roll of book paper and feather and green glass glitter. Add dimensional magic to each bottle to adhere the contents securely in the bottle.

•Handy Hint•

Allow the dimensional magic in the bottles to dry before replacing cork stoppers.

You can add scents and herbs to the bottles for extra special look.

You could change the colors to pinks and whites for a shabby chic look.

Ribbon Spool Angel

Get the kids involved and create this heavenly angel to add to your Christmas decorating this year.

MATERIALS

2 30 x 30 cm (12 x 12 in) sheets of white cardstock

½ sheet of light weight chipboard

1 ribbon spool

1 toilet roll insert

Prima Julie nutting mixed media riley doll and wings stamp

Jet black archival ink

Gold glitter

White glitter

Dimensional magic

Pearl paint

Black rhinestones

1 large self-adhesive pearl

5mm self-adhesive pearl strips

Doily border punch

Tim Holtz mini snowflake rosette die

White eyelash fiber

White muslin

White feathers

White organza ribbon

Water spritzer bottle

Decorative rhinestone

Scalloped and nested circles dies

Embossing folder

Fine black pen

Flesh, yellow and caramel alcohol pens

Large bamboo skewer

Hot glue gun

Heat gun

Hand die-cutting machine

Scalpel

Glue stick

STEPS

- Cut 2 strips of teal cardstock 7 x 30 cm (2.8 x 12 in) punch border punch along one side. Score every 1 cm (0.5 in) and adhere together. Fold concertina style, adhere both ends together. Squash and adhere together as a rosette.
- Die-cut the rosette in red cardstock, fold concertina style, adhere the ends, squash down and adhere small card circle over top with hot glue gun to make a rosette.
- Dry brush gesso over top of both rosettes. Brush dimensional magic over outer edges of rosettes and sprinkle with white glitter, shake off excess and adhere together. Wrap white eyelash fiber around the red rosette.
- Die-cut label in white and blue, ink edges of white panel and adhere together. Adhere to front of rosette.
- Trim two strips from red cardstock 2.5 x 6 cm (1 x 2.3 in), cut a large V in one end. Cover with dimensional magic, smooth out with your fingertip and sprinkle over red glitter. Shake off excess and allow to dry. Tuck under label and adhere in place.
- Dab all over the number one with versamark, sprinkle over gold embossing powder and heat set. When cool adhere to one side of the label
- Dab black ink over arrow, cover with dimensional magic and allow to dry. Adhere button, sequin star and sparklet below the number 1. Layer over arrow and rhinestone heart.
- Cut 6 20 x 11 cm(8 x 4.5 in) panels, fold in half to form a 10 x 11 cm (4 x 4.5 in) card. Die-cut with a large circle die. Make sure you move the edge of the die a little over the folded edge, so you cut a circular folded card.
- Adhere each card together, dry brush gesso around edges. Wrap navy ribbon around red cards. Cut another circle in teal, and adhere to back of red cards, covering the navy ribbon.
- Adhere rosette to front cover of mini album and tie up ribbon.

•Handy Hint•

This makes a wonderful Christmas mini album, just add Christmas colors and papers.

Use glitter cardstock, to save time.

Cut photos out with a die too so they fit nicely into the album.

Some Bunny Loves You Explosion Box

Explosion boxes are always so much fun to make, you can put just about anything inside them for a sweet surprise

MATERIALS

1 30 x 30 cm (12 x 12 in) cream, white and pink Cardstock

1 15 x 15 cm (6 x 6 in) square of green cardstock

1 10 x 10 cm (4 x 4 in) chipboard

1 sheet of Graphic 45 'A time to Flourish April' cut apart patterned paper

2 small paper roses

1 medium paper rose

2 packets of adhesive pearl strips

1 Large adhesive pearl

White and pink adhesive pearls

Silver plastic trim

Green and silver eyelash fiber

2 small heart pins

Nested ovals die

Scalloped ovals die

Doily border punch

Nested and scalloped squares

Couture Creative vintage branch and bow ties dies

Bunny die

Silver glitter spray

White glitter

Dimensional magic

Small flower punch

Pearlescent poppy dew drop inks

Green tea dew drop inks

Sahara sand dew drop inks

Ocean depth dew drop inks

3 cotton buds

Vintage pink and turquoise glimmer mist

Double sided tape

3-D foam tape squares

Hand die-cutting machine

Hot glue gun

Metal ruler

Scalpel

Small stylus

Mouse pad

Small alphabet stamps

STEPS

- Die-cut 4 large ovals, and 1 large square from cream cardstock, score bottom of ovals at 2 cm, fold and adhere around 4 sides of the square, ink edges with Sahara sand.
- Die-cut 1 square from pink cardstock and adhere over top of ovals on the base.
- Die-cut 4 white scalloped ovals and 4 pink ovals, in the smaller sizes, ink edges of white ovals with Green tea ink. Adhere to the 4 sides in layering the pink ovals over the white.
- Roughly cut images from the patterned paper and die-cut with a smaller nested oval. Spray with glitter and adhere to each of the four sides with 3-D foam tape. If you wish, stamp a greeting onto one of the ovals before adhering down.
- Die-cut a scalloped square from cream cardstock, ink edges with green tea ink, adhere to base with 3-D foam tape. Wrap fibers around sides and secure in place with glue.
- With green cardstock die-cut 2 vintage leaves, affix to base in the center. Cut lots of fine strips from cream cardstock with a metal ruler and scalpel. Gather together and scrunch up. Unfurl and then twist into a nest by tying a loose knot, tucking the ends under each other. Adhere with hot glue onto a circle of scrap cream cardstock. Spray with glitter and allow to dry before attaching to the center of base.
- Die-cut 2 bunnies, one from white cardstock and one from chipboard. Adhere the white bunnies to either side of the chipboard. Apply dimensional magic to the bunny and smooth out with your fingertip. Sprinkle over with white glitter and adhere a small pink pearl as an eye. Dry and repeat on the other side. Adhere the bunny to the center of nest with hot glue.
- Dip 3 cotton buds in glimmer mists, and roll into white glitter and allow to dry. Snip off the tops to form an egg shape, adhere to nest with hot glue. Affix the 3 paper flowers and tuck in 2 heart pins. With a dry bristle brush rub poppy ink into center of flowers, make sure you do not have too much ink on the brush for a gentle look.
- Punch 3 small flowers from white cardstock, cup the centers with a stylus and mouse pad, add small pearls to the centers and affix to side of square.
- Trace lid template onto another sheet of cream cardstock, score on fold lines and assemble. Use wide double-sided tape to secure the sides of the lid.
- Die-cut a square from pink cardstock and adhere to the inside of the box. Die-cut 2 small scalloped ovals. Cover with dimensional magic, smooth out with your fingertip and sprinkle with white glitter. When dry attach one to inside lid with 3-D foam tape. Trim out 'EASTER' tab, ink edges and affix to inside lid with 3-D foam tape. Attach a medium pearl either side.

- Punch out doily border from white cardstock, trim to fit all four sides and adhere to inside edge of box.
- Cut 3 strips of pink cardstock 30 x 2.5 cm (12 x 1 in), spray with glitter spray and adhere to bottom outside of box and outside of lid. Apply adhesive pearl strip to bottom edge of lid.
- Die-cut a scalloped square from white cardstock and adhere to top of box. Die-cut a smaller Nested square from patterned paper and adhere to top of box with 3-D foam tape. Apply pearls around the edge.
- Attach second glittered scalloped oval to top of box with 3-D foam tape.
- Die-cut bow, from pink cardstock, assemble smaller and large bow, and adhere together, attaching two ends underneath to form a double bow. Spray with glitter and dry. Attach to top of box. Add silver trim and a pearl to center to finish.

•Handy Hint•

Using Dimensional magic to adhere glitter is better than glue as it is self-levelling and the glitter sinks into the fluid to give very little glitter shed later.

Tuck small chocolate eggs into the nest instead of the bunny if desired.

You can adapt this box to any theme.

Add a little glitter spray to the outside and inside of the box too. Not too much though, as it will yellow the papers.

Spool Photo Holder

Recycle ribbon or thread spools to make gorgeous photo pegs, great for the teacher, Dad or Granny.

MATERIALS

½ 30 x 30 cm (12 x 12 in) sheet of black cardstock

1 spool of old ribbon or thread spool

Black flat spray paint

'Live Laugh Love' mini chipboard words

Alphabet letters

Gold embossing powder

Aged linen Distress ink stamp pad

Embossing stamp pad

Black eyelash fiber

1 medium cream paper rose

2 small cream paper rose

1 30 x 30 cm (12 x 12 in) sheet old book page

1 30 x 30 cm (12 x 12 in) sheet old sheet music

Scalloped and nested circle dies

Couture Creations Kalani musical notes die

3mm pearl self-adhesive strips

Praline glitter

Musical notes brad

White organza ribbon

Pave self-adhesive stones

Hot glue gun

Paper coated wire

Small wooden peg

Hand die-cutting machine

Heat gun

Double sided tape

3-D foam tape

STEPS

- Spray paint ribbon spool with flat black spray paint.
- Cut two small scalloped circles from book paper, ink edges and adhere to top of spool. If you can, pull spool apart and adhere the second circle to the bottom of the spool.
- Photocopy the old sheet music onto copy paper, ink edges, trim and adhere to center of spool.
- Add pearl strips to the edges of the spool as pictured.
- Die-cut 2 music notes die from black cardstock, apply dimensional magic to the top, smooth out with your fingertip, and sprinkle with black glitter. Allow to dry and adhere around the spool.
- Apply the embossing stamp pad fluid to chipboard words, sprinkle over gold embossing powder and heat set. When cool adhere to spool with hot glue.
- Die-cut a small nested circle from white cardstock, cover with dimensional magic again, smooth with your fingertip, sprinkle with praline glitter. Allow to dry and adhere to top of spool with 3-D foam tape. Wrap a little black eyelash fiber around.
- Spray a length of paper coated wire and small peg with black spray paint. Adhere the peg upside down to the top of the wire. Insert into center of spool.
- Adhere music chip letters to top of peg. Die-cut a photo, sand edges, and adhere to a black die-cut scalloped circle and insert into peg.
- Adhere paper roses around the base of the wire and add a small musical brad to the side.
- Tie a small bow, add a decorative gemstone and adhere the wire stem below the peg.

•Handy Hint•

If you cannot find a ribbon spool you like, make one from chipboard and toilet roll inserts, spray with black spray paint.

This little project is so inexpensive you can make it in any theme, music, English, maths or sports, for all of the teachers.

Create the same thing in Christmas colors for a gorgeous gift or placecard. Use photos of all of your guests and place above their plate.

Add some large glass beads or stones into the base if you want it to be heavier.

Spring Seedling Punnet

This is the perfect gift for the gardener in your life, and a wonderful way to organize your spring seeds.

MATERIALS

1 30 x 30 cm (12 x 12 in) chipboard sheet

1 30 x 30 cm (12 x 12 in) sheet of brown cardstock

5 30 x 30 cm (12 x 12 in) sheets of cream cardstock

1 30 x 30 cm (12 x 12 in) Websters Gardner's Seeds patterned paper

1 10 x 10 cm (4 x 4 in) white cardstock

Script stamp

Sepia archival ink stamp pad

Large white paper rose

White glitter

Praline glitter

Spray adhesive

Dimensional magic

3 small paper flowers

6 paper leaves

Petaloo burgundy berries

Wood grain embossing folder

Scalloped and nested oval dies

3mm self-adhesive pearl strips

White brads

Caramel alcohol pen

Gesso

Metallic gold paint

Corner rounder punch

Small alphabet chipboard

Melted chocolate dylusions spray ink

Small alphabet stamps

Hot glue gun

Hand die-cutting machine

Heat gun

Bamboo skewer

Crop-a-dile hand punch

Double sided tape

3-D foam tape

STEPS

- Use template for library pocket to make up 12 pockets, score and fold, adhere tabs with double sided tape. Randomly stamp with script stamp and sepia ink. Ink the edges also.
- Trim out seed panels, round edges with corner punch, and ink with sepia ink. Adhere to fronts of seed packets.
- Cut all of the brown cardstock into 2 cm (0.8 in) strips, also cut the chipboard into 2 cm strips. Emboss the brown cardstock with wood grain embossing folder.
- Dry brush brown cardstock wood grainm and chipboards strips with gesso. When dry spritz with chocolate dylusions and dry with heat gun. Apply gold paint over raised areas with your fingertip or a dry brush.
- Fold 4 strips of the brown cardstock at 5 cm (2 in) and then 15 cm (6 in) and again at 20 cm (8 in) to form a U shape. Adhere chipboard to the back of the strips, cutting the chipboard at 5 cm (2 in), 15 cm (6 in) and 20 cm (8 in) folds so the strip can be folded nicely.
- Fold 4 strips at 2 cm (0.8 in), 12 cm (5 in), 22 cm (8 in) and 24 cm (9 in) then trim off excess. Adhere chipboard strips to the back of the 12 cm and 22 cm section, leaving the 2 cm tabs on each end free. Adhere two of the strips together overlapping the tabs to create 2 square shapes.
- Using hot glue adhere U shaped pieces around the outside of the 2 square shapes.
- Punch holes where the panels overlap and insert a brad, color brad with a brown or caramel alcohol pen.
- Take excess brown wood grain cardstock, and cover the inside of the panels to hide the backs of the brads and give the box more strength. No need to cover the bottom panels.
- Die-cut a medium scalloped oval from white cardstock and a nested oval from a scrap of patterned paper. Apply dimensional magic to the edge of the white scalloped oval, sprinkle with praline glitter and allow to dry.
- Stamp the patterned oval with the word 'GARDEN', and adhere over glittered oval with 3-D foam tape. Adhere little chip letters over top. Snip up pearl strip and carefully adhere around the edge of the oval and attach to front of punnet with 3-D foam tape or hot glue.
- Spray white rose with adhesive, dip into a pot of white glitter, twirl wire stem around a bamboo skewer and affix to side of oval.
- Add in smaller flowers, petaloo berries and small leaves to decorate.

•Handy Hint•

This punnet does not have to be accurate, in fact, the more rustic, the better.

Cutting the chipboard on the folds, allows the panels to fold up nicely, it would not do this if you just glued them down without the cut.

You can add real images from old seed packets to the front of the pockets if you cannot find an appropriate patterned paper.

You could also do this without the wood embossing folder, or consider scoring in wood grain lines with a mouse pad and stylus.

Sweet Dreamcatcher

Create this delightful dream catcher for any new additions to your family. The soft colors will suit a nursery for either a boy or girl.

MATERIALS

1 30 x 30 cm (12 x 12 in) sheet of white cardstock

1 30 x 30 cm (12 x 12 in) sheet of blue cardstock

½ 30 x 30 cm (12 x 12 in) sheet of chipboard

Tim Holtz crescent moon and stars die

Small feather die

Nested circles dies

Orange micro beads

Alphabet chipboard letters

Chipboard word

3mm self-adhesive pearl strips

Large self-adhesive pearls

Black rhinestones

White pearls

1 large pearl bead

White glitter

Dimensional magic

White eyelash fiber

Embossing folder

Embossing stamp pad

Pale blue stamp pad

Pearl string

Sunshine yellow dylusions spray

Gesso

Pearl paint

Bamboo skewer

Hot glue gun

Heat gun

Hand die-cutting machine

Double sided tape

Crop-a-dile hand punch

STEPS

- Die-cut 2 large circles from chipboard, layer over a small circle die and re cut to form 2 frames. Repeat this step with white cardstock too.
- Cut 7 strips of blue cardstock approximately 1 x 10 cm (0.5 x 4 in) and adhere randomly across one of the chipboard circles to form the dream catcher supports. Trim edges if needed.
- Adhere the 2 chipboard pieces together and the 2 white circles on the front and back. Ink edges lightly with pale blue ink.
- Apply dimensional magic over the entire surface, smooth out with your fingertip and sprinkle with white glitter, repeat for the other side and allow to dry. Wrap edges with white eyelash fiber.
- Die-cut crescent moon and 5 stars from chipboard, and then die-cut 5 stars from white cardstock. Adhere white stars over chipboard ones, layer surface with dimensional magic and sprinkle with glitter, adhere a large pearl to the centers.
- Paint crescent moon with gesso, dry with heat gun, then cover surface with dimensional magic and sprinkle with micro beads, allow to dry.
- Paint moon with gesso again, until you can no longer see the orange color of the beads, dry with heat gun. Spritz with yellow dylusions and dry again. Apply a little pearl paint over the edges and surface, also add a black rhinestone as an eye.
- Punch a hole in top of moon and adhere to the dream catcher circle.
- Thread pearl string through the hole and add a large pearl and tie off securely.
- Adhere glittered stars around the edges of the moon and dream catcher.
- Trim a 2.5 x 10 cm (1 x 4 in) strip of white cardstock, ink edges and roll up ends with a bamboo skewer.
- Apply embossing stamp pad over chipboard letters and word and sprinkle with gold embossing powder and heat set. Adhere letters to scroll and word to the base of the moon.
- Die-cut 6 feathers from white cardstock, adhere 2 together to form 3 sturdy feathers, insert sections of string in-between the layers. Allow to dry.
- Rub over with a little pearl paint, fold feathers a little to create dimension and apply pearl strips down the centers of feathers and a larger pearl to the top.
- When dry adhere to back of dream catcher with hot glue and trim to fit.

Sweet Stroller Party Favor

Instead of a card, make this sweet 3-D pram, fill with sweets, small gift soaps or baby jewellery and give to a new parent, they will love you to bits!

MATERIALS

1 30 x 30 cm (12 x 12 in) sheet pink cardstock

½ 30 x 30 cm (12 x 12 in) sheet of white cardstock

1 10 x 10 cm (4 x 4 in) green cardstock

White glitter

Dimensional magic

Pink blush self-adhesive pearls

White self-adhesive pearls

Large pearl brads

3mm small pearl strips

Pearl sprays

White pearl paint

White muslin

Doily border punch

Foliage die

Nested circles die

Couture Creations Penny Farthing die

2 medium pink paper roses

3 small pink rose buds

1 bamboo skewer

Hot glue gun

Hand die-cutting machine

Double sided tape

3-D foam tape

Crop-a-dile hand punch

STEPS

- Die-cut 2 of the largest circle from pink cardstock, trim in half.
- Cut a 6 x 30 cm (2 x 12 in) strip of pink cardstock, score a 1 cm (0.5 in) tab down the long side of the strip to create a long tab either side. Snip along the tabs every 1 cm (0.5 in) fold them up and shape into a curve.
- Using the hot glue gun to adhere the curved strips to one set of semi circles, trim off excess. This will make the bottom of your pram.
- Roll excess paper around a bamboo skewer and hot glue in place, trim and adhere to one end of the pram.
- Trim a 0.5 x 30 cm (0.2 x 12 in) strip, fold in half and adhere together, when dry adhere to the end of pram to form a handle.
- Die-cut 4 medium circles from pink cardstock, and 4 penny farthings from white cardstock. Snip off excess from the penny farthing to make 4 wheels. Cover with Dimensional magic, smooth out with your fingertip and sprinkle with white glitter. Allow to dry and adhere to pink circles and add a medium pink pearl to the center.
- Adhere each wheel to the sides of the pram with hot glue, be careful to line them up so the pram sits squarely.
- Punch 8 x 17 cm (3 x 6 in) strips of doily border from pink cardstock, layer over each other and punch a hole into the ends, insert brads and spread the lacy strips. This takes patience, as you space them hot glue them in place so they stay there.
- Punch a hole in the side of the pram, unfurl the brad and reset when inserted through the side of the pram. Repeat for other side and adhere second set of semi circles to the sides to cover the back of the brad. Add pearl trim to edge of bonnet.
- Trim out a small piece of white cardstock to fit as a blanket inside the pram, curl with your fingers to fit just on top of pram.
- Die-cut leaves with foliage die, dry brush pearl paint over the leaves and adhere to the white blanket. Layer over paper roses, pearl sprays and tuck shards of teased muslin into the cluster.

•Handy Hint•

Add a bamboo skewer to the inside of the wheels to make the pram more stable,

especially if you are putting a weighty item inside.

You can make this in blue or pink or any of the pastel baby colors.

If you don't have the penny farthing, just use several nested circles of different colors.

Add extra glue to the pearl strips, if they are not sticking around the curves well.

Fill the pram with a cute little plastic dolly.

Teapot Gift Box

Gift boxes don't get much more adorable than this miniature elegant teapot. Fill it with scented teas, for a beautiful gift for your mother.

MATERIALS

1 30 x 30 cm (12 x 12 in) sheet of white cardstock

1 10 x 10 cm (4 x 4 in) green cardstock

2 apricot paper flowers

Pearl paint

Pearl adhesive strips

Green beaded trim

Twig punch

Doily border punch

'With Love' stamp

Aged Linen Distress Ink stamp pad

White organza ribbon

1/16 hand hole punch

A4 embossing folder

Hot glue gun

Hand die-cutting machine

STEPS

- Draw 4 triangles onto cream cardstock using template and cut out. Score along fold lines to create tabs, ink all edges.
- Using smaller triangle template cut out 8 triangles from patterned papers (make sure not to cut out images needed later on) Ink edges and adhere to both sides of larger triangles, above the scored tab line.
- Place one triangle on Die-cutting machine plate, layer a medium oval over top and roll through to cut oval window. Ink edges of oval window.
- Cut a 10 x 10 cm (4 x 4 in) square from cream cardstock, ink edges and adhere all four triangles around the sides.
- Punch a hole in the top of each triangle. Using some scrap patterned paper, punch a small hole 8 times. Layer over 1 cm (0.5 in) circle punch so the smaller hole is directly in the middle and punch to create a decorative reinforcement. Adhere over punched hole in top of triangle.
- Cut a 10 x 10 cm (4 x 4 in) square of kraft cardstock to adhere the base and a smaller patterned paper one to layer over the top.
- Trim out borders from patterned paper, use blue teapots to adhere to inside bottom of 3 side triangles. Use the pink one to adhere to bottom of 3 front triangles, layer over pearl strips, leaving the oval window triangle for later.
- Fussy cut stamps and use scallop scissors to decorate the sides, adhere 3 to inside back panel with foam tape.
- Die-cut 2 scalloped ovals from cream cardstock, ink edges and adhere to other 2 side panels. Die-cut images from patterned paper, ink edges and layer over top with 3-D foam tape.
- Use more borders to decorate inside window triangle and fussy cut a Botanical tea badge and adhere to top of triangle.
- Punch Doily border from white cardstock, adhere to square base, with a mitre cut at each corner.
- Cut an 8.5 x 8.5 cm (3.5 x 3.5 in) square from patterned paper, ink edges and adhere over white lace with 3-D foam tape, affix pearl strips around the edges.
- Cut a 7.5 x 7.5 cm (3 x 3 in) squares and adhere over top with 3-D foam tape. Punch fence punch from white cardstock, fold to fit around smaller square and hot glue in place.
- Die-cut a window from chipboard, dab over versamark and sprinkle with white embossing powder, heat set and allow it to cool. Fussy cut flowers, and a butterfly, adhere to edges of window as pictured. Adhere window inside fence with hot glue. Cut out the tea party tab, curl with a bamboo

skewer and just insert over fence.

- Die-cut tree from chipboard, ink with gingerbread ink both sides and adhere against the back of white fence. Trim off excess branches if needed.
- Die-cut the victorian lady from chipboard and 2 more from scraps of patterned paper. Adhere the papers to either side of lady. Snip patterned shapes in half and alternate on opposite sides. Draw in hair and eyes, add a few pearls to the top of hat and also adhere to center of box with hot glue.
- Use template and left over patterned paper to create with a small packet, decorate with fussy flowers and insert a scented tea bag. Tuck in between tree and lady.
- Fussy cut extra flowers, borders and Botanical tea badge for the front of the box, ink edges and adhere in place as pictured.
- Tuck teased muslin amongst tree, lady and window. Add pearls around outside oval window, by snipping up strips to curve around oval. Punch out daisies from white cardstock and adhere around window and front of box, add yellow glitter glue to the centers and allow to dry.
- Tie organza ribbon through the eyelets at the top to finish.

•Handy Hint•
Use a mouse pad and stylus to cup fussy cut images and add depth.

Trinket Box

Create this delightful trinket box to nestle a precious piece of jewellery into for someone special in your life.

MATERIALS

Small paper mache box

1 30 x 30 cm (12 x 12 in) sheet of black cardstock

Aged Silver embossing powder

Embossing stamp pad

1 paper rose

Bubblegum dylusions spray ink

Water mister bottle

3mm pearl adhesive strip

Black eyelash fiber

Couture Creations peacock fans embossing folder

Spellbinders Shapeabilities Asian Motifs die

Couture Creations Everyday essentials strawberry leaf die

Small scrap of acetate

Green metallic paint

Black flat spray paint

Heat gun

Hot glue gun

Hand die-cutting machine

Double sided tape

3-D foam tape

STEPS

- Spray paper mache box with black spray paint and allow to dry.
- Die-cut 2 of the large squares from the Asian set, from black cardstock.
- Swipe over versamark embossing stamp pad, and sprinkle with Aged silver embossing powder, shake off excess and heat set.
- Adhere both squares to the top and bottom of the box.
- Emboss remaining black cardstock with Peacock fans folder.
- Swipe over versamark and sprinkle with Aged silver embossing powder, shake off excess and heat set.
- When cooled, cut embossed panel up to fit the sides of the box.
- Cut a square 6.5 x 6.5 cm (2.5 x 2.5 in) from embossed panel, adhere to top of box with 3-D foam tape.
- Apply pearl strip around the edge of square.
- Die-cut 2 leaves from green cardstock, dry brush with metallic green paint and adhere to top of box.
- Spray Bubblegum dylusions onto an acetate sheet, spray white flower with water, and dip the edges of the petals into the puddle of bubblegum dylusions. Do this until you have the look and intensity you desire, also dip into Silver embossing powder and heat set.
- Adhere flower to top of box and wrap black eyelash fiber around the flower.

•Handy Hint•

You can make this in gold too, however don't try to be too neat with the embossing powder as you want that old beaten metal look.

If you have too much embossing powder on the die-cut shape, just use a brush to remove some.

If you cannot find a box to suit, consider cutting down a taller one.

Up, Up and Away

This 3-D hot air balloon gift can be made in any color or theme, just fill the little basket with sweets for a wonderful keepsake.

MATERIALS

Prima Cartographer, Montogolfier, Marveilleux, Postale patterned paper

1 30 x 30 cm (12 x 12 in) Black cardstock

3 Prima Cartographer flowers and leaves

½ sheet 30 x 30 cm (12 x 12 in) inch Teal cardstock

16 large enamel dots

Black glitter

Dimensional magic

Black eyelash fiber

Silver spray glitter

3mm self adhesive Pearl strips

White adhesive pearls

Jet Black Archival ink

Double arches border punch

Bamboo skewers

Small blue pony beads

Couture Creations siblings, Albert & Simonetta, and Party banner dies

Square nested dies

Decorative paper clip

Alphabet stamps

Double sided tape

3-D foam tape squares

Hot glue gun

Hand die-cutting machine

STEPS

- Cut 4 balloon panels from patterned papers and the box template from black cardstock using templates provided.
- Ink edges of balloon panels and adhere all four together with double sided tape, lining up the spines and trimming the edges to match if needed. Do not adhere the tabs at the bottom together.
- Assemble box, trim edges if needed. Die-cut 8 panels from patterned papers, ink edges and adhere 4 to outside of box with 3-D foam tape. Adhere the remaining 4 to the inside of the box with double sided tape.
- Punch black cardstock with border punch and adhere to top of outside box, cut a thin strip of teal cardstock and overlay the black border. Affix a strip of pearls over that.
- Adhere 4 skewers to the insides of the box, secure with a hot glue gun. Snip to leave about 7 cm of skewer above the box.
- Adhere balloon tabs over skewers, using hot glue and trim if needed. Punch out more black cardstock with border punch and adhere over balloon tabs. Layer over a thin strip of teal cardstock and pearls. Adhere small pony beads to tops of skewers and add a small adhesive pearl to the top of each.
- Fussy cut 2 hot air balloons from patterned paper and attach to top of balloon and to the bottom box.
- Cluster flowers over fussy cut balloon on the bottom box, adhere with hot glue, and tuck in leaves and black fibers.
- Cut 8 banners from black cardstock and adhere to sides of balloon with hot glue, crossing them over each other. Cut thin strips of teal cardstock and curl around a bamboo skewer, trim and attach to the edge of the balloon over end of each banner. Place a large enamel dot over each end.
- Trim a 1.5 x 10 cm strip of teal cardstock, scrunch up, and unfurl and fold in half, stamp a word of you choosing on to each side, adhere together, tucking a bamboo skewer into the middle. Cut a large V into the end and insert into the middle of Balloon. Tuck decorative paper clip over one edge of balloon. Spray a little of the spray glitter over the flag and balloon area.
- Die-cut siblings and Albert and Simonetta twice each, glue both pieces together to make a strong shape. Apply dimensional magic over each and smooth out with your finger, sprinkle with black glitter allow to dry and repeat with the other side.
- Tuck each of the figures around the edge of the box and secure in place with hot glue.

Valentines Heart Tealights

These delightful Valentines party favours are so quick and easy to make you will be able to share the love with lots of family and friends.

MATERIALS

1 30 x 30 cm (12 x 12 in) sheet of white cardstock

1 30 x 30 cm (12 x 12 in) sheet of pink or red glitter paper

1 30 x 30 cm (12 x 12 in) cm green cardstock

9 red tea lights

Red patterned washi tape

Small pink paper rose

Leaf punch

Scalloped and nested heart dies

Spray adhesive

White glitter

Pearlized twine

Small white bow

Small red heart sequin

2 mm (0.8 in) bubblegum gemstones

Hot glue gun

Hand die-cutting machine

Glue stick

Cello bags

STEPS

- Die-cut 9 scalloped hearts from white cardstock.
- Die-cut 9 nested hearts from glitter paper, adhere glittered hearts over top of scalloped hearts with glue stick.
- Wrap washi tape around each of the 9 tea lights.
- Adhere each candle to the center of the glittered heart.
- Add a small bow to the front of the candle, and attach the sequin heart.
- Carefully apply the 2 mm gemstone to the center of the heart sequin.
- Pack the heart and candle into cello bags, tie up with pearl twine.
- Punch leaf punch from green cardstock, adhere this along with rose to the tied bag.

•Handy Hint•

Hot glue will adhere the candle quickly and easily.

Die-cut a smaller heart and adhere to the back of the white scalloped heart, so you can write a greeting on it.

There is no need to take the candle off the glittered heart while burning.

Never leave a burning candle unattended.

Violet Ribbon Spool Candle Holder

This beautiful candle holder is so economical to make, you can make several of them to adorn the center of your table for any occasion.

MATERIALS

1 30 x 30 cm (12 x 12 in) sheet of white cardstock

Patterned floral paper

Large ribbon spool

1 10 x 10 cm (4 x 4 in) green cardstock

Doily border punch

Leaf punch

Nested and scalloped circles die

Hand die-cutting machine

Hot glue gun

Double sided tape and 3-D foam tape

3 velvet violets

Purple paper rosebuds

White eyelash fiber

Petaloo purple/lavender berry clusters

White glitter

Dimensional magic

4mm pearl self-adhesive strip

Small white bow

STEPS

- Remove the top of the ribbon spool. Die-cut 2 scalloped circles from white cardstock. Take one and layer over a smaller nested circle about the same size as the pillar on the spool. Die-cut so you now have a donut shape.
- Adhere the donut shape to base of spool and re-adhere the card top to the spool. Brush dimensional magic around the edge of the second scalloped circle and dip into white glitter, adhere over top of the card top.
- Trim patterned paper to cover the pillar, and adhere in place around the center.
- Die-cut 2 nested circles from white cardstock, one larger than the other. Adhere both of these circles to the top of the spool with 3-D foam tape.
- Punch 4 strips of doily border from white cardstock, adhere one at the base of the pillar, and one at the top, with 3-D foam tape. Carefully adhere another strip around the larger circle on the top and the last one around the smaller circle as pictured.
- Adhere medium pearl strip around the edge of the bottom strip on the top.
- Wrap white fibers around the pillar at the bottom.
- Die-cut another smaller scalloped circle from white cardstock, brush over dimensional magic, smooth out with your fingertip and dip into a pot of white glitter.
- Adhere to front of ribbon spool with several layers of foam tape.
- Gather 3 velvet violets into a bunch, adhere a small bow to the front, affix a pearl to the center. Attach the bunch to glittered circle.
- Punch out leaf punch from green cardstock and tuck into violets, trim small roses and add into cluster. Snip off excess from berry stems and adhere in place in the cluster.
- Add a slim white candle to finish.

•Handy Hint•

If you don't have a ribbon spool, make your own with toilet roll holders and chipboard die-cut circles.

If you don't have circle dies, use jam jar lids as a template to cut out circles. Use deckle scissors on the edges instead of scalloped dies.

These can be made in any color scheme or theme to suit any occasion.

Welcome Swallow Window Ornament

What better way to say welcome to a friend, than this hanging faux cloisonné swallow.

MATERIALS

Sizzix songbird die

½ 30 x 30 cm (12 x 12 in) sheet of light weight chipboard

1 10 x 10 cm (4 x 4 in) white and green cardstock

Flourish embossing folder

Twig punch

Assorted beads

Gold liquid pearls

Small alphabet stamps

Jet black archival stamp pad

Ocean depth dew drops stamp pad

Medium white paper rose

Gold thread

Small paper doily

Black rhinestones

Dimensional magic

White glitter

Gesso

Calypso teal dylusions

Squeezed orange dylusions

Hot glue gun

Hand die-cutting machine

Double sided tape

Heat gun

Crop-a-dile hand punch

STEPS

- Die-cut swallow twice from chipboard. Emboss one of the swallows with embossing folder and adhere over the other swallow.
- Paint with gesso, allow to dry and apply a second coat.
- When dry, spray swallow with teal dylusions and add a small amount of orange to the throat of the swallow, dry with a heat gun.
- Apply dimensional magic over the entire surface, add a very light sprinkle of white glitter and allow to dry.
- Add a small rhinestone for the eye, and use gold liquid pearls to pick out the swirly design of the embossing folder. Also apply liquid pearls around the edge of the bird.
- When dry, punch a hole in top of swallow, thread through gold string with several beads attached.
- Adhere swallow onto a paper doily.
- Trim a 10 x 1 cm (4 x 0.5 in) strip of white cardstock, scrunch up and unfurl. Stamp 'WELCOME' onto cardstock with black ink and ink edges with Ocean Depth stamp pad.
- Punch 2 leaves from green cardstock, adhere to base of bird along with a white paper rose to finish.

•Handy Hint•

This makes a wonderful Christmas decoration. This swallow is so easy and economical to make, you could cover your tree in birds.

If you don't have an embossing folder, just do random swirls with the liquid pearls.

Wishing Well Centerpiece

For something different, make this tiny wishing well as a table centerpiece for a wedding or baby shower. Fill it with money or lucky tickets for the bride or mother to be for an added surprise.

MATERIALS

Floral patterned paper

1 30 x 30 cm (12 x 12 in) square of pink and green cardstock

½ 30 x 30 cm (12 x 12 in) sheet of white cardstock

½ 30 x 30 cm (12 x 12 in) sheet of chipboard

1 small pringle tin

Fine tip black pen

Dimensional magic

2 large paper roses

6 small pink paper roses

1 decorative hat pin

White eyelash fiber

Spray adhesive

gesso

White glitter

String

Melted Chocolate dylusions spray

White Linen dylusions spray

Pearlescent poppy dew drops stamp pad

3mm pearl adhesive strip

Blush adhesive pearls

Bubblegum 2 mm (0.08 in) gemstones

Bunny brads

Butterfly brads

Couture Creations Vintage branch die

Couture Creations Garden Lamp die

Couture Creations Party Banner die

Scalloped and nested circles dies

Grass border punch

Flourish embossing folder

Bamboo skewer

Craft foam bird and plastic mushrooms

Plastic basket buttons

Hot glue gun

Hand die-cutting machine

Heat gun

Crop–a–dile hand punch

STEPS

- Cut the pringle tin to a suitable size and paint with gesso.
- Trim chipboard into small brick like pieces, no need to be too accurate but about 1.5 x 1 cm (0.6 x 0.4 in) will do nicely. Adhere around the edge of the tin with hot glue and paint again with gesso.
- Spray with chocolate dylusions and dry with heat gun. Flick white line dylusions around the edges and ink with pearlescent poppy.
- Die-cut 2 large scalloped circles in white cardstock, adhere one to the bottom of the tin. Punch grass border from green cardstock and adhere to bottom of tin, wrap with fibers and adhere in place.
- Cut two 2 x 12 cm (0.8 x 5 in) strips of chipboard, emboss with embossing folder and ink with Poppy ink, adhere to the inside sides of the tin.
- Die-cut 6 vintage branches from green cardstock and adhere to sides and up the edges of the supports.
- Spray two large flowers with spray adhesive and dip into a pot of white glitter, shake off excess and adhere over vintage branches on both sides along with the six pink roses.
- Adhere bunny, mushrooms and butterfly around the leaves. Add some small 2 mm (0.08 in) gemstones as tiny flowers.
- Die-cut a circle that fits inside the tin from remaining patterned paper, and trim out the center, snip into two and adhere along the rim to hide it. Affix small pink pearls over top.
- Punch two holes into the sides of the supports and thread through a bamboo skewer and trim to fit.
- Wrap around the string and attach the baskets and bird.
- Cut 2 slits into the second scalloped circle and affix over the supports.
- Cut two strips of patterned paper 5 x 30 cm (2 x 12 in) each, score at every 1 cm and concertina fold up. Adhere both together and at each end to form a circle. Squash together to form a rosette and hot glue together to form a rosette. Ink the folds.
- Hot glue to the top of well, add decorative hat pin and wrap fibers around the join of the scalloped circle and rosette top.
- Die-cut 4 garden lamps, adhere 2 together to form a stronger shape, color the lamp with a black fine tip pen and coat with Dimensional magic, and sprinkle with a little white glitter. When dry attach to the sides of the roof and add a small pearl.
- Die-cut 2 party banners, ink edges, add pearl strips and attach to the sides of the roof as well.

Templates

Mini Carousel book Template

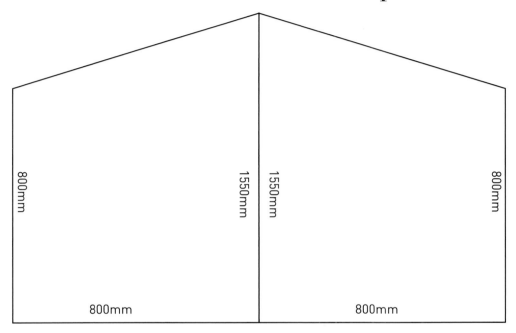

800mm

1550mm

1550mm

800mm

800mm

800mm

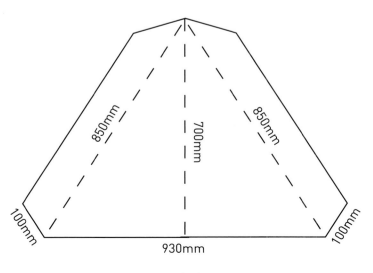

850mm

700mm

850mm

100mm

100mm

930mm

Easter Box Template Lid only

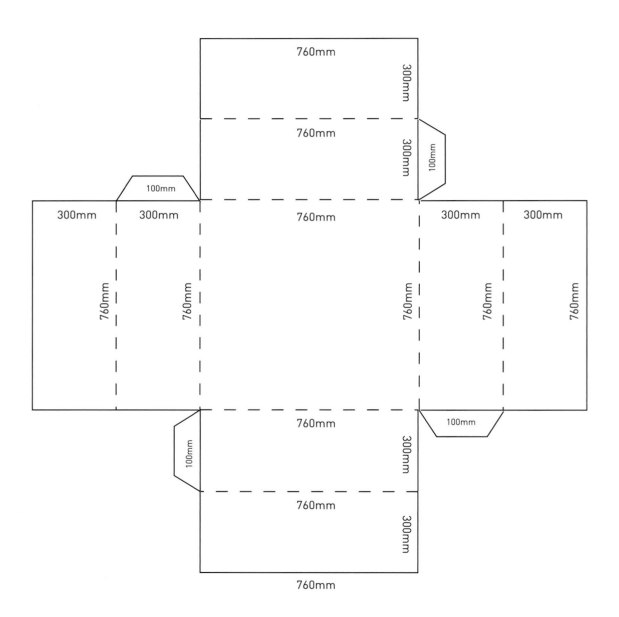

760mm

300mm

760mm

300mm

100mm

100mm

300mm | 300mm

760mm

300mm | 300mm

760mm

760mm

760mm

760mm

760mm

760mm

760mm

760mm

100mm

100mm

760mm

300mm

760mm

300mm

760mm

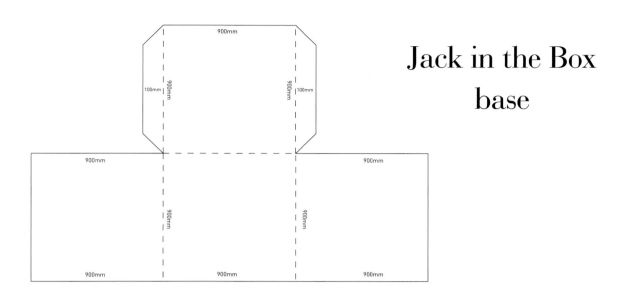

Jack in the Box base

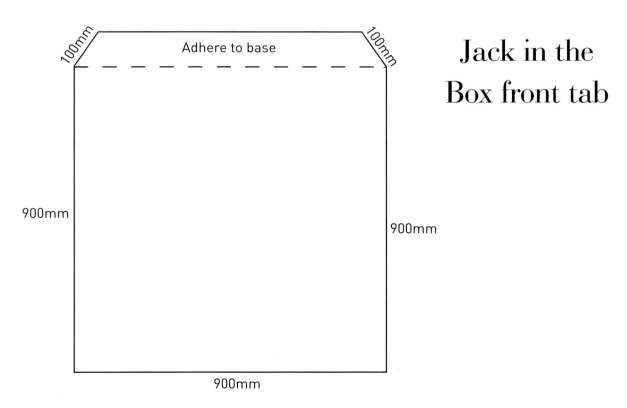

Jack in the Box front tab

Jack in the Box Template Top

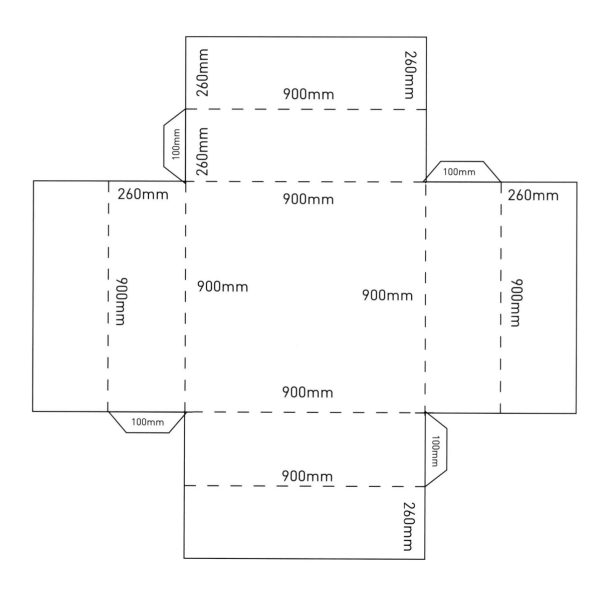

Up, Up and Away balloon template

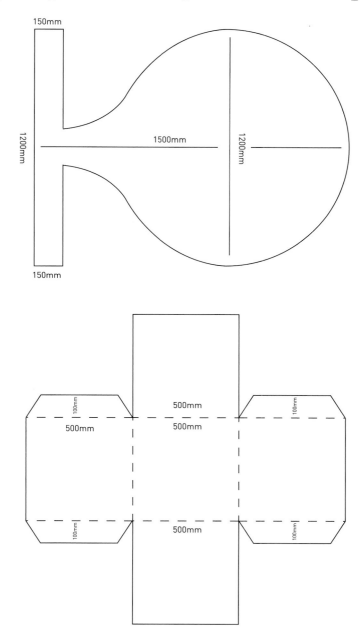

150mm

1200mm

1500mm

1200mm

150mm

100mm

500mm

500mm

500mm

500mm

100mm

100mm

500mm

100mm

Door Hanger Template

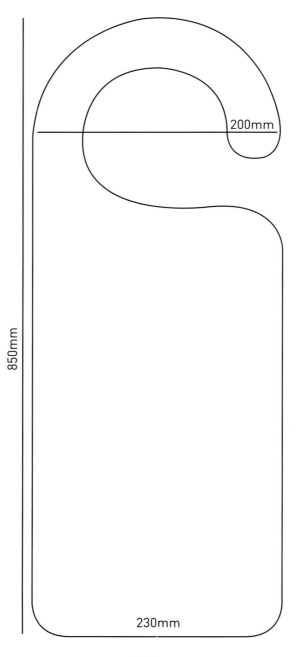

200mm

850mm

230mm

Birdhouse Template

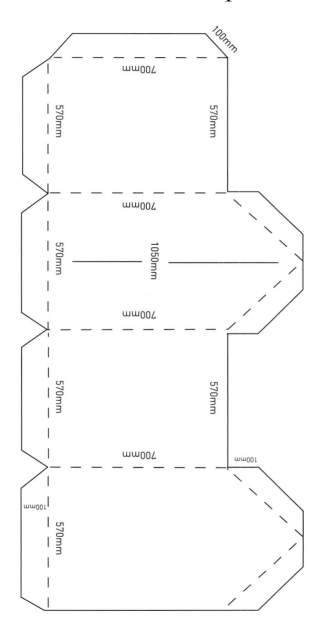

Elf Boot Template

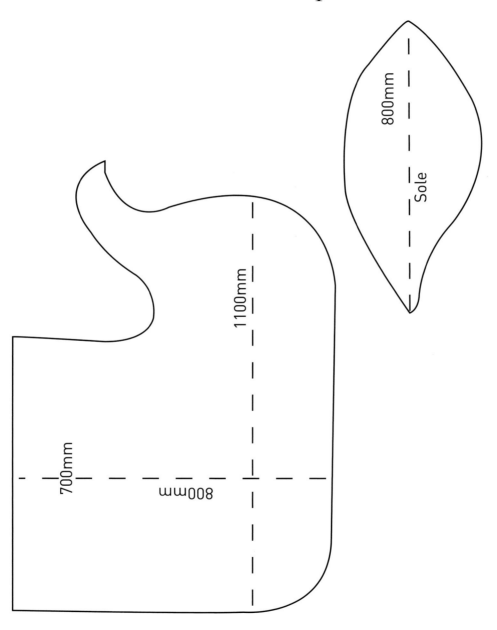

800mm

Sole

1100mm

700mm

800mm

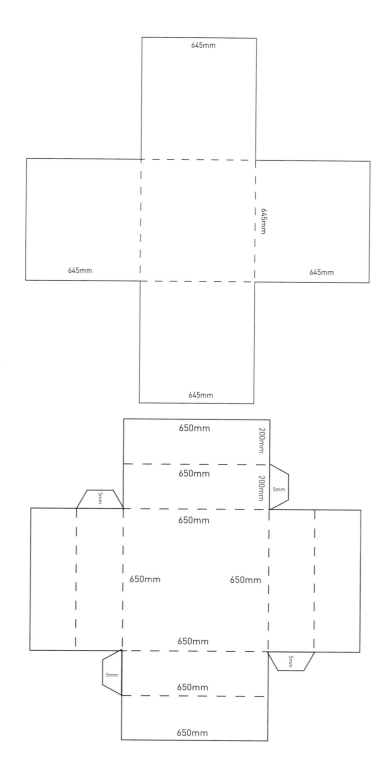

Base for Happy Birthday Box

645mm

645mm

645mm

645mm

645mm

Top of Happy Birthday Box

650mm

200mm

650mm

200mm

5mm

5mm

650mm

650mm

650mm

5mm

650mm

5mm

650mm

650mm

Mini Cupcake Template

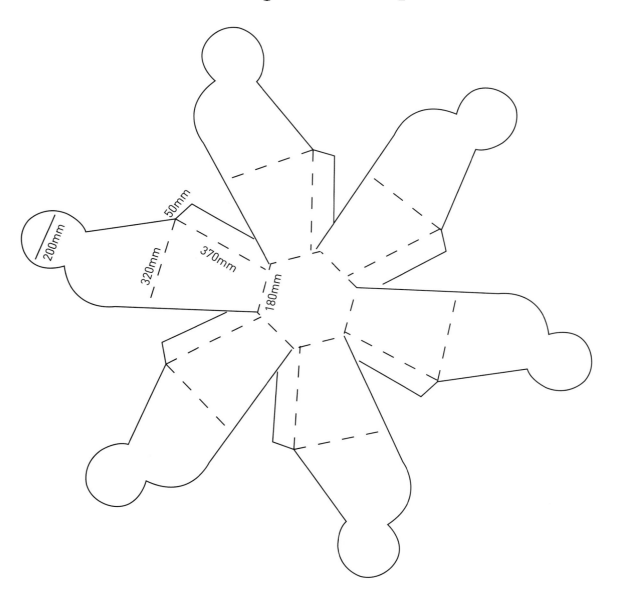

50mm

200mm

320mm

370mm

180mm

Mother's day Pop up Box Base Template

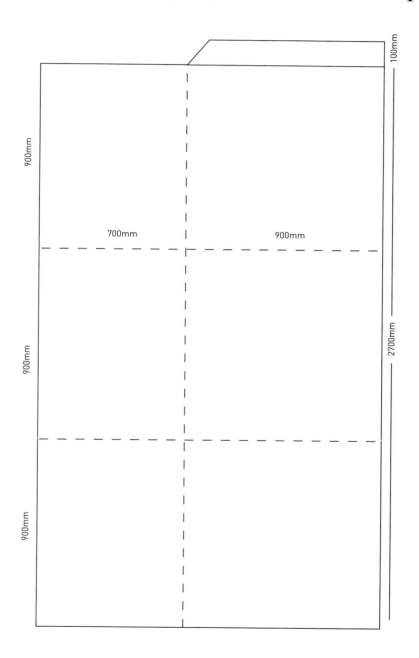

Mother's day Pop up Box add on Template

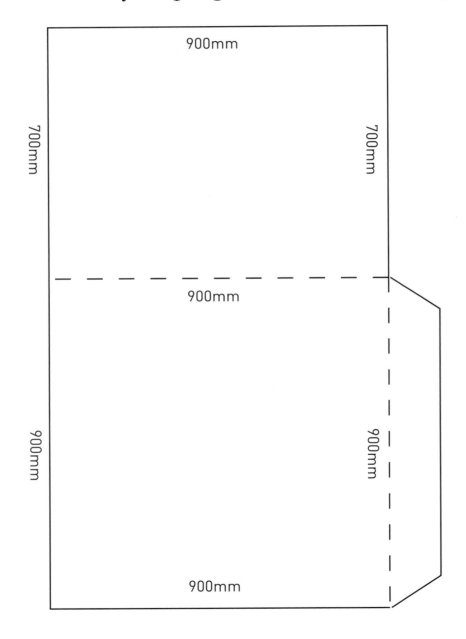

900mm

700mm

700mm

900mm

900mm

900mm

900mm

Owl Treat box Template

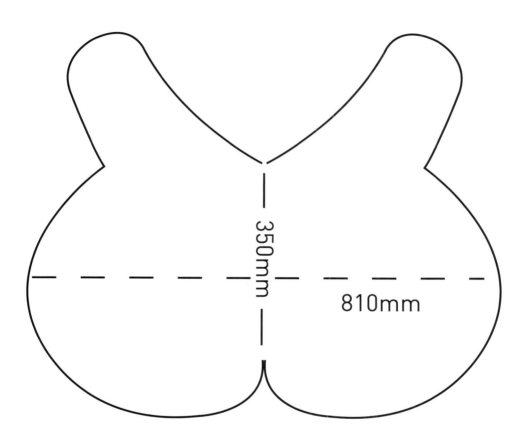

350mm

810mm

Piece of Cake Base Template

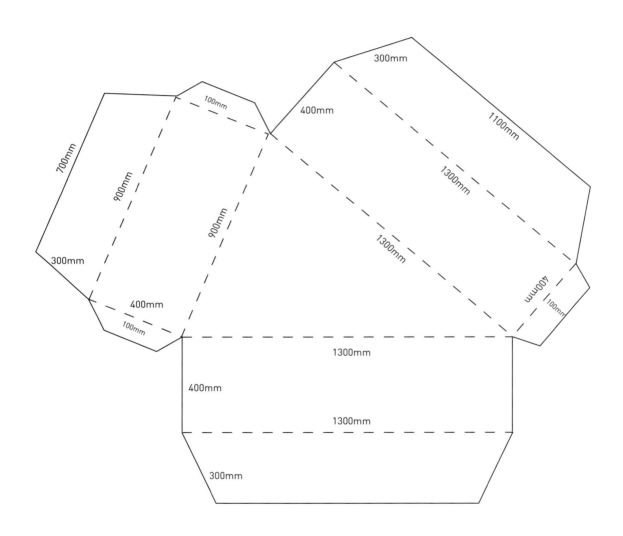

Piece of Cake Top Template

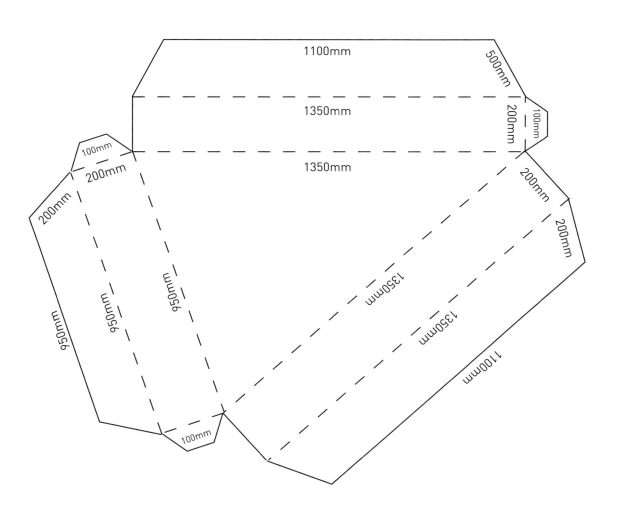

Seedling Punnent Packet Template

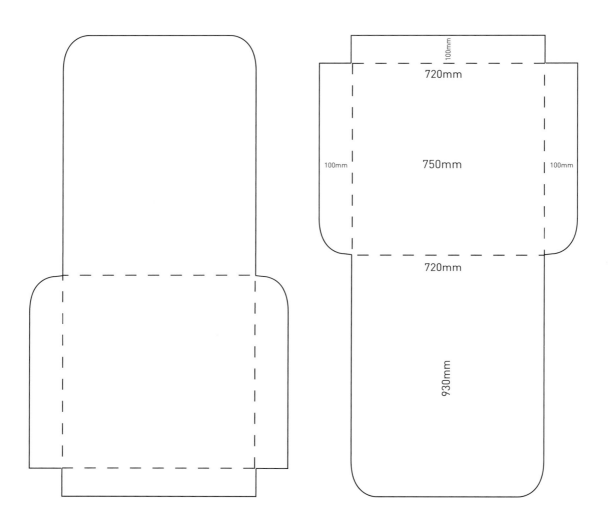

Snowglobe Base Template

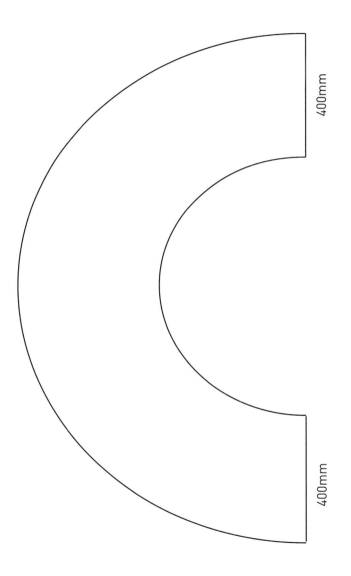

400mm

400mm

Teapot Gift box Template

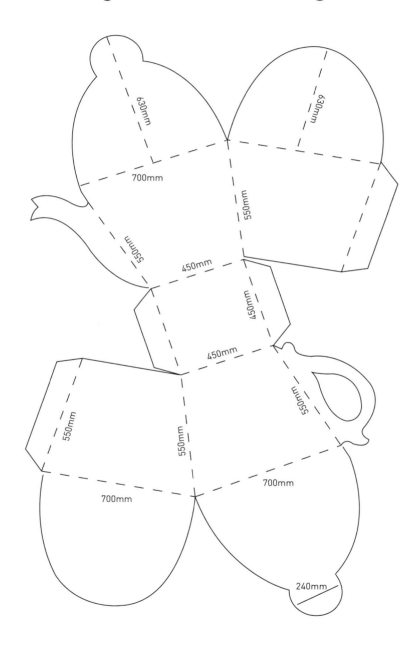

630mm

630mm

700mm

550mm

550mm

550mm

450mm

450mm

450mm

550mm

550mm

550mm

700mm

700mm

240mm

Time for Tea Pyramid Box Template

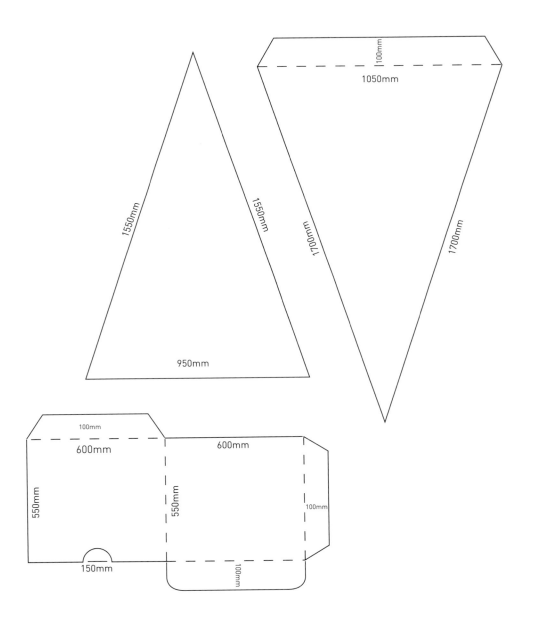